GREEK COOKING

Ruth Kershner

WEATHERVANE
BOOKS

PICTURE CREDITS

The following picture was provided through the courtesy of Transworld Feature Syndicate, Inc.:
Syndication International p. 11

contents

introduction

The cuisine of Greece is steeped in 3,000 years of history. It is influenced by the land itself, by the seas, and by the various conquerors who have occupied her shores. Those peoples who have visited her shores and traveled on have left behind some contributions from their homelands. The food is well-prepared and robust. While it may lack the subtlety of the haute cuisine of France, it is highly varied and aptly shows the ingenuity of the people. It represents a crossroads of Eastern and Western cuisine and culture. Being on the trade routes between Europe and Asia, it contains elements of both while remaining Mediterranean in character.

Let us first consider some of the contributions of the ancient peoples. Olives and grapes were cultivated by the ancient Greeks. As long as 3,000 years ago, olive oil and wine were an integral part of the diet. The famous retsina (resinous wine) of Greece is said to have originated during ancient times. The wine was stored in goatskin bags, then the bags were smeared with pitch to stop leakage and preserve the wine. The people became so accustomed to the taste imparted by the pine resin, that even today it is added to the wine.

The Greeks of ancient times were of necessity a seafaring people and returned from their trading voyages with many improvements to their way of life. The art of beekeeping was learned in Egypt and brought home to Greece. Today the honey of Hymettus is still some of the sweetest in the world. With the fall of the ancient Greek civilization, many of their culinary discoveries passed on to the ancient Romans and into our cuisine today.

At various periods in history all or part of Greece was ruled by the Bzyantine Empire, the Venetians, and the Turks. The Golden Age of Bzyantine cuisine was during the sixth century under Emperor Justinian and Empress Theodora. Theodora had many chefs and brought to her court the cuisines of India, Persia, Greece, Syria, and Cyprus. Through the influence of the Byzantine Empire, the basis of the present-day foods of Greece, Turkey, and the Middle East were formed. Theodora encouraged trade with Asia. Rice, lemons, and eggplant were introduced from India and are still important in the diet. The flaky, thin pastry of Persian origin known as phyllo was introduced through the influence of Theodora's court. Stuffed grape leaves also were introduced during this period.

The Venetians brought with them macaroni and other pasta products, tomato-based sauces, and Eastern spices, for Venice had a monopoly on the spice trade at that time. To this day cinnamon, allspice, aniseed, pepper, and cloves are used lavishly in Greek cooking.

The Ottoman Empire was in control of Greece from 1460 until 1821. Although the Turkish rule caused a great deal of animosity, many Turkish customs were adopted by the Greeks. The most noteworthy custom is the preparation of coffee. A finely pulverized coffee is added to the water in a long-handled brass pot. Sugar is added to taste during preparation. It is served in small cups with a glass of pure, cold mountain water, for which the Greek countryside is known. The cuisines of Greece and Turkey today are quite similar. The pastries and sweets, for example Turkish Delight, are relished in both countries. Yogurt was introduced by the Turks, as well as the ubiquitous kabobs.

Greek food, as that of any country, is limited by the land and conditions. Modern Greece encompasses some 50,000 square miles, of which only one-fourth is arable. The soil is poor and the terrain rugged. Cliffs seem to rise from the sea. There are almost 10,000 miles of coast, dotted with shallow harbors. Hundreds of islands also comprise the nation, a number of which are isolated and accessible only by sea.

Cattle, and thus beef and veal, are rare in Greece, as grazing land is poor and not plentiful. Sheep and goats provide the bulk of the meat and milk that are used. Chickens are plentiful, but generally only mature birds find their way to the table. Pork is not commonly eaten. The Turks, who are Moslem, may have influenced the tastes of the Greeks in this respect.

Fresh vegetables are highly prized, since meat is expensive. Any family having a small plot of land grows its own supply. Tomatoes, peppers, onions, artichokes, beans, cauliflower, and broccoli all are favorites. Wild greens are collected and cooked or served in salads. In a country where wild herbs abound, oregano, rosemary, dill, mint, parsley, fennel, and thyme are collected and used in abundance. A pot of fresh basil grows in every window, but not for eating. It is the symbol of hospitality, and sprigs are presented to guests as a gift.

With such an extended coastline, seafood is a staple of the diet and many kinds are eaten. Lobster, clams, mussels, red mullet, scallops, and much more comprise the day's catch and find their way into the stewpot.

Greece is still basically a rural country. Electricity is gradually being brought to the rural areas, but is by no means universal. Refrigeration is not commonly found in homes outside of large urban centers. Most homes have no oven and only a kerosene or charcoal stove. For this reason soups and stews are frequently eaten. Roasts are spit-roasted over charcoal, and many meats are grilled. Bread is an extremely important part of the diet, and the local baker performs another important service. After the day's bread is baked, villagers bring in casseroles and cookies to be baked for a small charge. Since these items are then picked up and transported home for the main meal of the day, main dishes are not hot when eaten but are lukewarm. Salad vegetables are marinated in vinegar and oil and served at room temperature, rather than chilled. Milk is quickly made into cheese to prevent spoilage in a warm climate and is served frequently in the diet.

Since 96 percent of the population of Greece is of the Greek Orthodox religion, religious beliefs play an important role in food-consumption. Feast days occur frequently and are celebrated with special meals. Easter is the principle religious celebration of the year, preceded by a strict observance of Lent. The Lenten fast of 40 days is broken at midnight on Holy Saturday with Mageritsa, a soup made from lamb innards. A baby lamb is then spit-roasted on Easter for dinner. Namedays, rather than birthdays, are celebrated with cookies and other sweets from the Zaharoplastia (confectioner). Christmas is celebrated with an exchange of gifts on January 1, St. Basil's Day. Weddings and baptisms are lavishly celebrated occasions of great joy.

The Greeks lead a leisurely Mediterranean life and meals reflect this attitude. Breakfast at 6:30 or after is usually light and continental in character, consisting of tea or boiled milk and bread. Lunch is generally eaten between 1 and 3 in the afternoon and is the main meal of the day. Meat, poultry, fish, a pilaf or stew with salad, bread, fruit or a plain dessert, and Greek coffee constitute the meal. Siesta prevails from dinner until about 4:30 P.M. Coffee and pastry are eaten at the Kafeninion (coffee house) in the late afternoon. Supper is eaten quite late at night, generally around 10:00 P.M.

After the day's work is completed, the men gather in the taverns for a drink of ouzo, wine, or beer and mezes (appetizers), for the Greek never drinks without eating. Appetizers can range from plain to very elaborate and may include olives, tomatoes, feta, cucumbers, pickled squid, taramosalata, meatballs, dolmathes, and savory phyllo pastries, all served with crusty bread. This is a time of relaxation and conversation for the Greek, and appetizers play an important role in their social life. Dinner is then served at 10 or later, with fruit, cheese, and nuts for dessert, followed by Greek coffee.

Ouzo, straight or with water, is the national beverage. It is strongly anise-flavored and ranges from 80 to 100 proof. Wines are very popular, retsina being by far the most popular. Retsina can be white, rosé, or red and it is said that the taste must be acquired. Beer is also produced in Greece and is quite good. Citro and Masticha are liquers of a unique character. The alcoholic beverages of Greece are unique in taste and well worth trying.

Greek cuisine is extremely adaptable, since no special pots, pans, or utensils are required. Many of the recipes could be used for outdoor cooking, adding to their versatility. The recipes are equally adaptable for an everyday meal or company feast, with only small additions needed. The Greek meal, as you can see, is really a "movable feast," infinitely variable and adaptable. It is cooked "analogos," or to the liking of the cook. Recipes are passed from mother to daughter and rarely written down, making each dish a new experience, since every cook has her own tastes. It is a new and exciting pleasure offered here for you to try. Please feel free to adapt and experiment to make these recipes a part of your permanent collection. Good cooking and good eating!!!

guide to unusual ingredients

Feta is a white goats-milk cheese. It is slightly salty in taste, since it is cured in brine and crumbly in texture. It is available in Greek and Italian delicatessens and in large supermarkets, where it may be packed in jars or cans. Save the brine to pour over the cheese when storing it.

Kafaloteri is a hard, grating cheese made from ewe's milk. A well-aged Parmesan or Romano cheese, grated just before each use, would substitute well.

Kasseri is a ewe's-milk cheese that is semi-hard. A good New York State aged cheddar would substitute very well in casserole dishes. However, do not substitute cheddar for Kasseri in the fried cheese hors d'oeuvres, as it melts too easily. Kasseri is available in Greek and Italian delicatessens and is cut from a large wheel.

Mizithra is a goat cheese that can be hard or soft in nature, depending on how long it is dried. It is unique in flavor and, if available, very interesting to taste. Serve it as a table cheese or grate it over macaroni, where it is superb. Mizithra has been referred to as "the queen" of cheese. You will not find this cheese in a recipe in this book, since it is generally imported and difficult to obtain unless you live near a large Greek community. If it is available, substitute it for Kasseri cheese on macaroni.

Bulgur wheat is cracked wheat and is available in specialty shops in the gourmet sections of most large supermarkets.

Fides are long, very thin vermicelli noodles. They are available in Italian groceries, or the more common vermicelli can be substituted.

Grape-vine leaves may be picked fresh, but are more commonly available packed in brine in cans and jars. Do not substitute.

Mint. Fresh spearmint grown in a pot makes a delicious addition to Greek recipes.

Olives are generally black and shriveled and pickled in brine. Greek olives are available in most delicatessens.

Olive oil. Use a good quality Greek or Italian olive oil to assure good flavor.

Oregano is used frequently in Greek cooking and should be crumbled before using. In Greece it is referred to as "rigani" and is a form of wild marjoram. Oregano is the closest herb in taste that is readily available.

Orzo is a rice-shaped noodle, generally available in Italian grocery stores. It is commonly used in soups. If you cannot buy it, simply substitute rice.

Pine nuts are generally available in Greek or Italian groceries or in gourmet shops. If you cannot find them, substitute blanched slivered almonds, browned in butter.

Rice. Any long-grain white rice may be used. If converted rice is used, check the package directions for the amount of liquid required in cooking. Do not use precooked rice.

Salonika peppers are hot peppers resembling Italian pickled hot peppers. Substitute the Italian hot peppers on appetizer trays or in salads, or simply omit them.

Phyllo is paper-thin pastry used in baking. The size is generally around 16 × 18 inches per sheet, with many sheets to the pound. If your phyllo is a different size, trim it to fit the baking pan, allowing more sheets if necessary. Phyllo is always brushed with butter — generally sweet butter, but salted butter may be used for some main dishes. Phyllo must always be covered until ready to use. Work with only one sheet at a time, covering the rest of the phyllo with plastic wrap or tea towels. If phyllo is unavailable, frozen puff pastry, thawed and rolled very thin, may be substituted. Frozen strudel leaves are the same as phyllo. Homemade strudel also may be used. Any leftover phyllo should be wrapped well and frozen.

Tarama is carp roe and is available in speciality stores in cans and jars.

appetizers

caviar dip
taramosalata

½ of an 8-ounce jar of tarama
1 small onion, finely grated
1 egg yolk

4 slices white bread (stale)
¼ cup lemon juice
½ cup olive oil

Place the tarama in a blender jar and whirl at low speed to a smooth paste. Add the onion and egg yolk and whirl to mix.

Remove the crust from the bread and soak the bread in water. Squeeze to dry. Tear it into pieces and add to the fish-roe mixture. Whirl until well-blended. Add the lemon juice and olive oil alternately while whirling at medium speed. Blend at high speed until well-combined.

Chill and serve with melba toast, pita bread, or lavash (Arabic crisp flatbread) and crisp raw vegetables. Makes 1½ cups.

pickled onions
kremmithakia marinata

1 pound small boiling onions
½ cup water
½ cup white wine
½ cup olive oil

Juice of 2 lemons
½ teaspoon salt
10 peppercorns
1 small bay leaf

Peel the onions and make an "X"-shaped cut in each end to keep them from splitting.

Combine the water, wine, oil, lemon juice, salt, peppercorns, and bay leaf in a medium-size saucepan. Bring to a boil, then reduce the heat and simmer for 5 minutes. Add the onions and cook over low heat for 25 minutes or until tender.

Cool the onions and serve them in a bowl with a small amount of the pan liquid. Serve with cocktail picks. Makes 6 to 8 servings.

picture on opposite page:
stuffed grape-vine leaves,
caviar dip, and pita bread

stuffed grape-vine leaves
dolmadakia

Dolmadakia can be frozen in a covered container. Thaw it in the refrigerator for 24 hours before serving.

1 1-pound jar vine leaves	parsley
1½ tablespoons olive oil	½ teaspoon salt
1 medium onion, finely chopped	Freshly ground pepper
½ cup pine nuts	½ teaspoon cinnamon
¾ cup raw long-grain rice	2 medium tomatoes, peeled, seeded, and chopped
½ cup golden raisins	Juice of 1 lemon
2½ cups water	¼ cup olive oil
2 tablespoons finely chopped	Lemon wedges for garnish

Unfold the vine leaves and rinse them carefully under cold running water. Drain them.

Heat the 1½ tablespoons of oil in a saucepan. Add the onion and sauté until limp. Add the pine nuts and cook over medium heat for 5 minutes. Add the rice, raisins, and 1½ cups of the water. Cover and cook for 20 minutes or until all liquid is absorbed. Stir in the parsley, salt, pepper, cinnamon, and tomatoes.

With the stem end of the leaf toward you, place approximately 1 tablespoon of filling on each vine leaf. Fold up the stem end to enclose the filling. Fold the sides to the center and roll to form a neat package. Do not try to secure the rolls with toothpicks, as they are fragile and will tear easily.

Place a thin layer of unfilled vine leaves in the bottom of a large, heavy saucepan. Tightly pack the rolls in the pan, seam-side-down, in layers. Sprinkle each layer with some of the lemon juice and part of the ¼ cup of oil. Add the remaining 1 cup of water and place a heavy kitchen plate on top of the rolls in the pan to weight them down. Cover the pan. Bring the rolls to a boil, then reduce the heat to simmer and cook for 30 minutes. Remove from the heat and cool.

Carefully remove the stuffed leaves from the pan and serve them cold garnished with lemon wedges. Makes 6 servings.

stuffed clams
kydonia yemista

2-dozen clams (little-neck or rock)	½ cup raw long-grain rice
¾ cup dry white wine	¼ teaspoon pepper
¼ cup water	½ teaspoon allspice
½ teaspoon salt	¼ teaspoon cinnamon
3 tablespoons olive oil	3 tablespoons currants
½ cup chopped onion	3 tablespoons pine nuts
	2 tablespoons chopped parsley

Scrub the clams and soak them in several changes of cold water to remove the sand. Place in a skillet with the wine, water, and salt. Cover and steam for 10 minutes, until the shells open. Discard any clams that do not open. Cool and then remove the clams from the shells. Save the shells and strain the pan juices.

In a medium saucepan heat the oil and sauté the onion until golden. Add the rice and 1 cup of the pan juices. Bring to a boil. Cover and reduce the heat to low. Cook for 15 minutes. Add the pepper, spices, currants, pine nuts, and parsley. Cook for 5 minutes. Cool.

Dice the clams and add to the pilaf.

Stuff the shells with the rice mixture and chill. Serve as an appetizer. Makes 24 appetizers.

spinach and cheese pies
spanakopittes

1 egg
½ medium onion, finely
   chopped
¼ pound crumbled feta cheese
4 ounces cream cheese
5 ounces (½ of a 10-ounce
   package) frozen chopped
   spinach, thawed and
   drained

1 tablespoon chopped parsley
½ teaspoon dillweed
½ teaspoon garlic powder
6 sheets phyllo or 4 frozen
   patty shells (omit the butter
   when using the patty shells)
1 stick butter, melted

In a blender or mixer bowl combine the egg, onion, and feta cheese. Beat to combine. Add the cream cheese and combine well. Add the spinach and seasonings and mix just until blended. Chill for 1 hour.

phyllo dough

Phyllo must be handled with great care, since it is very delicate and dry to the touch. Carefully unroll as many sheets as you need and store the remainder immediately. Place the sheets not immediately in use between linen tea towels to prevent drying. If the weather is very hot and dry, sprinkle a little water on the towels.

Phyllo sheets are generally 16 × 22 inches. Stack 2 leaves together, cutting through both sheets. Cut strips 2 inches wide by 16 inches long. Brush with melted butter. Place a teaspoon of filling on one end of the strip. Fold one corner of the strip to the opposite side, forming a triangle and enclosing the filling. Continue folding as you would an American flag, to the end of the strip, maintaining the triangular shape. Brush with melted butter.

Place on an ungreased cookie sheet and bake at 375°F for 20 minutes. Serve hot.

puff pastry dough

Defrost the patty shells at room temperature for 15 to 20 minutes. Form each shell into a ball and roll on a floured pastry cloth to an 11 × 11-inch square. Cut into 16 individual squares. Place ½ teaspoon of filling on each square. Fold to form a triangle, and seal with milk. Bake at 450°F for 12 minutes. Makes approximately 33 if made with phyllo, approximately 64 smaller pastries if made with puff pastry dough.

Note: These can be baked and then frozen. Reheat on a cookie sheet at 350°F for 15 minutes.

shrimp pies
psaropetes

4 ounces cream cheese
1 egg yolk
1 tablespoon chopped parsley
1 tablespoon chopped green
   onions
½ teaspoon lemon juice
¼ teaspoon salt

1 6-ounce package small
   frozen shrimp, thawed and
   chopped
2 tablespoons grated
   Kafaloteri (or Parmesan)
   cheese
6 sheets phyllo
1 stick butter, melted

Whip the cream cheese with an electric mixer. Beat in the egg yolk. With a spatula mix in the parsley, green onions, lemon juice, salt, shrimp, and cheese. Chill for 1 hour.

Proceed as for Spinach and Cheese Pies (see above recipe), using the phyllo dough or substituting the puff pastry. Makes 30 appetizers.

soups

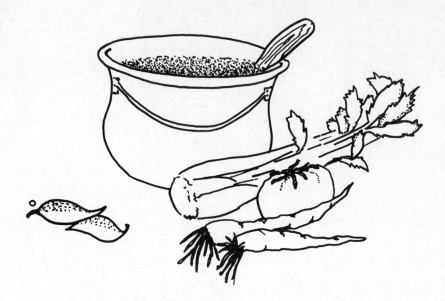

egg and lemon soup with meatballs
giouvarlakia avgolemono

1 pound lean ground beef or
  lamb
¼ cup raw long-grain rice
¼ cup finely chopped onion
2 tablespoons finely chopped
  parsley
Salt and pepper
2 10½-ounce cans chicken
   broth
2 soup-cans water
2 eggs
⅓ cup lemon juice
Parsley for garnish

Combine the beef, rice, onion, parsley, and salt and pepper to taste.
Shape into small meatballs, using a rounded teaspoon of the meat mixture
for each one.

In a 3-quart saucepan, combine the chicken broth and water and heat to
boiling. Add the meatballs, cover, and reduce the heat to simmer. Cook
for 20 minutes.

Beat the eggs until thick and lemon-colored. Slowly beat in the lemon
juice. Now add 1 cup of the soup broth slowly to the egg and lemon
mixture, while continuing to beat. Add the mixture to the soup in the
saucepan, and heat through.

Garnish with parsley and serve immediately. Makes 4 to 6 servings.

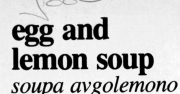

egg and lemon soup
soupa avgolemono

2 10¾-ounce cans
   condensed chicken broth
2 soup-cans water
2 teaspoons dried parsley

⅓ cup raw long-grain rice
2 eggs
Juice of 1 fresh lemon

Combine the chicken broth, water, and parsley. Bring to a boil. Add the rice. Cover and cook for 25 minutes.

Meanwhile, beat the eggs well. Slowly add the lemon juice to the eggs while continuing to beat. Slowly pour 1 cup of the hot soup into the egg mixture while beating. Slowly pour the egg and soup mixture back into the soup pot while stirring vigorously. Cook over very low heat for a few minutes, stirring constantly, until slightly thickened. *Do not boil,* as the mixture will curdle.

The chicken-broth mixture can be made in advance and reheated, but do not add the egg and lemon-juice mixture until just before serving. This soup does not reheat well.

Makes 4 servings.

meatball soup
giouvarlaki

soup stock
2 tablespoons olive oil
½ cup chopped onion
1 clove garlic, minced
2 10¾-ounce cans condensed beef
   broth
2 soup-cans water
½ cup red wine
3 tablespoons tomato paste

meatballs
1 pound ground beef
¼ cup raw long-grain rice
1 egg, beaten
¾ teaspoon crushed dried
   mint
½ teaspoon salt
¼ teaspoon pepper
2 tablespoons chopped fresh
   parsley for garnish

Heat the oil in a 3-quart saucepan. Add the onion and garlic and cook until limp. Add the beef broth, water, wine, and tomato paste. Bring the broth mixture to a boil slowly while making the meatballs.

Combine all the meatball ingredients, mixing well with your hands. Roll into small meatballs, using a rounded teaspoon of meat mixture for each one.

Drop the meatballs a few at a time into the boiling stock. Cover the saucepan and reduce the heat to low. Cook for 20 to 25 minutes or until the rice in the meatballs is thoroughly cooked.

Garnish with the chopped parsley and serve. Makes 4 servings.

chilled cucumber soup
taratori

¼ cup shelled walnuts
1 large clove garlic, peeled
3 tablespoons olive oil
1 tablespoon white wine
   vinegar
3 cups yogurt

⅓ cup cold water
1 cucumber, peeled and
   chopped
Salt and pepper
Chopped fresh mint or parsley

Combine the walnuts, garlic, oil, and vinegar in a blender container and blend at medium speed until smooth. The mixture may also be mashed together with a mortar and pestle.

Combine the yogurt and water in a mixing bowl and add the walnut mixture. Stir until all the ingredients are well-mixed. Add the cucumber and salt and pepper to taste. Chill for several hours before serving.

Garnish with fresh chopped mint or parsley. Makes 4 servings.

salads

seafood salad with mayonnaise
psari salata me mayoneza

3 cups cooked seafood (any one or a combination of crab, shrimp, or lobster)
½ cup chopped celery
½ cup sliced green onions
½ teaspoon dried dillweed

2 tablespoons olive oil
2 tablespoons lemon juice
4 medium tomatoes
2 hard-cooked eggs, sliced
Lemon wedges
Lettuce

caper mayonnaise
1 egg
½ teaspoon mustard
½ teaspoon salt
Dash cayenne pepper

½ teaspoon sugar
1 cup olive oil
3 tablespoons lemon juice
2 tablespoons capers, chopped

In a mixing bowl combine the seafood, celery, onions, dill, 2 tablespoons olive oil, and 2 tablespoons lemon juice. Mix well. Refrigerate until ready to use.

Slice the tops off the tomatoes. Scoop out the pulp and reserve for another purpose, leaving a shell approximately ½ inch thick. Drain.

Next, make the Caper Mayonnaise. In a blender container combine the egg, mustard, salt, pepper, sugar, and ¼ cup of the oil. Blend thoroughly. With the blender running, very slowly add ½ cup more oil. Then add the lemon juice gradually and the remaining ¼ cup of oil. Blend until thick, occasionally scraping the sides of the blender jar.

Transfer to a serving bowl and fold in the capers.

Arrange the lettuce on individual plates. Place one tomato shell on each plate and stuff with seafood mixture. Garnish with hard-cooked eggs and lemon wedges and serve with Caper Mayonnaise. Makes 4 servings.

cabbage salad
lahano salata

4 cups finely shredded
  cabbage
1 medium green pepper,
  shredded
2 tablespoons grated onion
1 teaspoon sugar

¼ cup vinegar
½ teaspoon salt
¼ teaspoon pepper
1 cup yogurt
½ cup mayonnaise
Green-pepper rings

Combine the cabbage, green pepper, and onion and toss well. Add the sugar, vinegar, salt, and pepper. Toss again and allow to stand for a few minutes.

Combine the yogurt and mayonnaise and add to the salad. Mix well and garnish with green-pepper rings. Makes 4 servings.

spinach salad with feta cheese
spanakosalata me feta

1 pound raw spinach
2 hard-boiled eggs, sliced
1 tomato, cut in wedges
½ medium onion, thinly sliced
½ cup crumbled feta cheese

salad dressing
6 tablespoons olive oil
2 tablespoons wine vinegar
½ teaspoon oregano
½ teaspoon salt
¼ teaspoon pepper

Wash the spinach well. Pick it over and discard any brown or damaged leaves. Remove the stems and break into pieces in a large salad bowl. Add the eggs, tomato, onion, and feta cheese.

Combine the dressing ingredients and shake well.

Pour the dressing over the salad, toss well, and serve. Makes 4 to 6 servings.

potato salad
patatasalata

4 medium potatoes
½ cup sliced green onions
1 teaspoon oregano
½ teaspoon salt

¼ teaspoon pepper
3 tablespoons wine vinegar
⅓ cup olive oil
2 hard-cooked eggs, chopped

Scrub the potatoes and cook unpeeled in boiling salted water for 30 to 40 minutes or until tender.

Cook, peel, and dice the potatoes. Add the onions, oregano, salt, pepper, vinegar, oil, and eggs and mix gently. Chill.

Serve the salad cold with meat or fish. Makes 4 servings.

tomato and cucumber salad with feta cheese
salata domates ke agouris me feta

1 large tomato, thinly sliced
½ medium cucumber, peeled
  and thinly sliced
½ cup thinly sliced Bermuda
  onion
3 ounces feta cheese, sliced or
  cubed

¼ cup olive oil
¼ cup wine vinegar
½ teaspoon crumbled
  marjoram
½ teaspoon seasoned salt

Arrange the tomato, cucumber, onion, and cheese in a small salad bowl.

Combine the olive oil, wine vinegar, marjoram, and seasoned salt and pour over the vegetables.

Let the salad stand at least 1 hour before serving. Makes 4 servings.

greek country salad

greek country salad
salata horitake

½ head iceberg lettuce
2 tomatoes, cut into wedges
½ medium onion, sliced and
   separated into rings
½ cucumber, sliced
¼ pound feta cheese, cut into
   ¾-inch chunks
3 anchovy fillets
½ cup calamata olives

salad dressing
⅓ cup olive oil
⅓ cup wine vinegar
2 tablespoons water
½ teaspoon dried dillweed

Break the lettuce into bite-size pieces and place in the bottom of a salad bowl. Top with the tomatoes, onion rings, sliced cucumber, cheese, anchovies, and olives.

Combine the dressing ingredients in a shaker bottle or plastic container and shake well.

Pour the dressing over the salad and toss just before serving. Makes 4 servings.

artichoke and tomato salad
salata marinata

2 4-ounce jars marinated
    artichoke hearts
½ cup sauterne
Juice of lemon
1 whole fennel
6 medium tomatoes, sliced
2 small onions, diced
1 clove garlic
½ teaspoon salt
¼ teaspoon white pepper
½ cup warm beef broth

Drain the artichoke hearts, reserving the marinade. Cut the artichoke hearts in half and place in a large salad bowl.

Combine the reserved marinade, wine, and lemon juice and pour over the artichoke hearts.

Clean the fennel, wash and slice, and add to the artichoke hearts. Add the tomatoes and onions.

Mash the clove of garlic with the salt and pepper and add to the beef broth. Mix well and pour over the vegetables. Marinate for at least 10 minutes.

Serve with crusty bread. Makes 6 to 8 servings.

Note: If fennel is unavailable, substitute 1 small bunch of celery, cleaned and sliced.

cucumbers with yogurt
angourosalata me yiaourti

2 medium cucumbers
1 medium red onion, sliced
¾ cup yogurt
1 teaspoon lemon juice
1 clove garlic, minced
¾ teaspoon salt
1 tablespoon chopped fresh
    mint

Score the skins of the cucumbers with the tines of a fork, and slice very thin. Place in a salad bowl with the red onion.

Combine the yogurt, lemon juice, garlic, and salt. Pour the mixture over the cucumbers and garnish with fresh mint. Chill for 1 hour before serving. Makes 4 servings.

zucchini salad
kolokythia salata

3 medium zucchini
1 medium onion, sliced and
    separated into rings
Juice of 2 lemons
    (3 tablespoons)
½ cup olive oil
¼ teaspoon oregano
¾ teaspoon salt
Chopped parsley

Wash the zucchini well under cold running water. Trim off the stem and slice very thin. Place in a large bowl. Cover with boiling water and let stand for 5 minutes. Drain well. Return to the bowl and add the onion rings.

Combine the lemon juice, oil, oregano, and salt and pour the mixture over the zucchini. Mix gently and marinate for several hours before serving.

Garnish with chopped parsley. Makes 4 servings.

meats

steak in the greek style

2 pounds sirloin steak (1 inch thick)
½ teaspoon freshly ground pepper

1 clove garlic, crushed
2 tablespoons lemon juice
½ teaspoon salt
1 teaspoon oregano

Rub the meat with pepper and garlic.

Broil or barbecue over medium-hot coals until done to your liking (15 minutes for medium). Sprinkle with lemon juice, salt, and oregano.

Slice across the grain and serve with the juices from the platter. Makes 4 to 5 servings.

tomato–meat sauce
makaronada

3 tablespoons butter
1 cup chopped onion
2 cloves garlic, minced
1 pound ground beef
1 6-ounce can tomato paste
2 cups water

¼ cup red wine
1 teaspoon salt
¼ teaspoon pepper
1 2-inch cinnamon stick
¼ teaspoon ground allspice
Dash ground cloves

Melt the butter in a large skillet. Add the onion, garlic, and beef and cook over medium heat, stirring occasionally, until the meat loses its pink color.

Combine the tomato paste and water and add to the meat mixture. Add the wine, salt, pepper, cinnamon stick, allspice, and cloves. Bring to a boil and then reduce the heat to simmer. Cook for 1 hour. Remove the cinnamon stick.

Serve over macaroni with grated cheese. Makes 4 servings as a main dish or 6 to 8 servings as a side dish.

savory pot roast
vothino entrada

1 4-pound pot roast
½ teaspoon salt
¼ teaspoon pepper
2 tablespoons flour
4 tablespoons butter
3 onions, sliced
3 carrots, peeled and sliced
2 stalks celery, sliced
½ cup tomato sauce
2 cups water
1 bay leaf
½ cup red wine

Wipe the meat with a damp cloth.

Combine the salt, pepper, and flour. Rub into the surface of the pot roast.

Melt the butter in a Dutch oven. Brown the pot roast on all sides. Add the onions and brown them. Add the carrots, celery, tomato sauce, water, bay leaf, and red wine. Cover and simmer for 3 hours.

Slice the meat and serve with the pan juices, accompanied by rice or potatoes. Makes 8 servings.

greek macaroni— meat bake
pastitso

3 tablespoons butter
½ cup chopped onion
1 clove garlic, minced
1 pound ground beef
¾ teaspoon salt
⅛ teaspoon pepper
¾ teaspoon cinnamon
¼ teaspoon sugar
4 tablespoons tomato paste
½ pound macaroni, cooked
¼ cup grated Romano cheese
1 egg

Melt the butter in a large, heavy skillet. Add the onion and garlic and cook until tender. Add the ground beef and brown it. Cover and simmer for 20 minutes. Add the salt, pepper, cinnamon, sugar, and tomato paste. Cook for 10 minutes.

Combine meat mixture, cooked macaroni, and Romano cheese. Stir well. Add the egg and stir to combine.

Turn the mixture into a greased 13 × 9 × 2-inch baking dish. Pack it down and make the surface level. Top with Custard Topping and dust with additional Romano cheese and cinnamon.

Bake at 375°F for 30 minutes or until the custard is set. Let stand for several minutes and cut into 8 squares to serve. Makes 8 servings.

custard topping

¼ cup butter
¼ cup flour
2 cups milk, warmed
2 eggs, beaten

Melt the butter and add the flour and stir until bubbly. Remove from the heat. Add the warm milk slowly, stirring well. Return the mixture to the heat, and cook, stirring constantly, until the mixture starts to thicken.

Slowly add the hot mixture to the beaten eggs while continuing to beat. Pour the mixture back into the saucepan and cook over low heat, stirring constantly, until the mixture becomes thick, like custard. If the mixture should form lumps, pour it through a fine sieve or puree it in a blender and then return it to the saucepan.

eggplant casserole

mousakas melitzanes

1 medium eggplant
  (1½ pounds)
1 pound ground beef (or
  lamb)
6 tablespoons vegetable oil

½ cup chopped onion
1 clove garlic, minced
1 8-ounce can tomato sauce
¼ teaspoon cinnamon
½ teaspoon salt

Peel eggplant and slice ¼ inch thick. Soak in salted water for ½ hour. Brown the ground meat in 2 tablespoons of the oil and remove from the pan with a slotted spoon.

Brown onion and garlic in the drippings. Add tomato sauce, cinnamon, salt, and the cooked meat. Simmer on low heat for 10 minutes. Set aside.

Drain the eggplant and dry it with paper towels. Place on a broiler pan in a single layer and brush with 2 tablespoons oil. Broil until brown. Turn and brush with remaining 2 tablespoons oil and brown under the heat source.

Layer the eggplant and meat sauce in a 2-quart casserole, ending with the meat sauce. Top with Rich Cheese Sauce and bake for 45 minutes at 350°F.

Leftovers are great reheated and served in pita bread pouches as a sandwich. Makes 4 servings.

rich cheese sauce

2 tablespoons butter
2 tablespoons flour
¼ teaspoon nutmeg
1 5¾-ounce can evaporated
  milk
¼ cup water

½ teaspoon chicken-broth
  granules
1 egg, beaten
1 cup cottage cheese, small
  curd
¼ cup Parmesan cheese

Melt the butter, and add the flour and nutmeg. Cook and stir until bubbly. Stir in the milk, water, and chicken-broth granules. Cook, stirring constantly, over low heat, until the mixture thickens and boils, about 1 minute.

Add 1 cup of the sauce slowly to the beaten egg and beat well. Then beat back into the mixture in the saucepan. Cook, stirring constantly, for 1 minute. Remove from the heat, stir in the cottage cheese and Parmesan cheese, force the mixture through a fine sieve, and use to top Eggplant Casserole.

pocket sandwiches

These sandwiches make a good winter dinner with lentil or split-pea soup.

2 tablespoons olive oil
1 pound ground beef or lamb
½ cup chopped onion
¼ cup chopped green pepper
½ cup tomato sauce

½ teaspoon salt
¼ teaspoon pepper
½ teaspoon crumbled dried
  oregano
4 pieces pita bread

Heat the olive oil in a medium-size skillet. Add the ground meat and sauté for 5 minutes. Add the onion and green pepper and sauté for 3 more minutes. Drain off the fat. Add the tomato sauce and seasonings. Cover and simmer for 5 minutes.

With a knife split the pita-bread pieces one-fourth of the way around and make a pocket. Stuff the bread with the meat mixture. Makes 4 servings.

stuffed cabbage leaves
lohano dolmathes

1 large head cabbage
½ pound ground beef
½ pound ground lamb
1 medium onion, chopped
1 clove garlic, minced
½ cup plain yogurt
½ cup raw long-grain rice
½ teaspoon crushed oregano
½ teaspoon salt

¼ teaspoon pepper
1 8-ounce can tomato sauce
2 bay leaves, crushed
1 10¾-ounce can beef broth
1 soup-can water
½ cup yogurt or sour cream
   mixed with chopped mint
   (for garnish)

Core the head of cabbage and place under running water. Peel off 12 large cabbage leaves. Save any leaves that break.

Put 1 inch of boiling water in a Dutch oven. Add the cabbage leaves and cover the pan. Steam over medium heat for 10 minutes or until the cabbage leaves are limp. Drain.

Mix the meats, onion, garlic, yogurt, rice, oregano, salt, and pepper. Fill the cabbage leaves with ¼ cup of the filling. Fold the 2 sides toward the center and roll tightly. Fasten with 2 wooden toothpicks.

Place the rolls in a large Dutch oven or skillet. Place any broken cabbage leaves on the bottom of the pot or slice any remaining cabbage and place under the cabbage rolls. Layer the rolls, placing tomato sauce and crushed bay leaf over each layer (there should be 2 layers). Pour the beef broth and water over the rolls. Cover the kettle and simmer for 1 hour.

Serve the cabbage rolls hot, garnished with yogurt or sour cream mixed with chopped mint. Makes 4 servings (12 cabbage rolls).

stuffed grape leaves with egg and lemon sauce
lohano dolmathes me avgolemono

⅓ cup olive oil
½ cup chopped onion
1 pound ground beef or lamb
¾ cup raw rice
1 tablespoon dried mint leaves
½ teaspoon salt
¼ teaspoon pepper
1 cup water
1 jar (1 pound) grape leaves
2 cups beef broth
   (approximately)

Heat the oil in a large skillet and sauté the onion until golden. Add the ground meat and sauté until it loses its pink color. Add the rice, seasonings, and water. Simmer covered for 10 minutes or until the water is absorbed. Remove from the heat and cool for 30 minutes before stuffing the grape leaves.

Drain the brine from the grape leaves and rinse under cold running water. Drain and pat dry. With the stem end facing you, place 1 tablespoon of the meat filling on the leaf. Fold the stem end up to cover the filling. Fold the sides in and roll.

Line a large skillet or saucepan with broken, unfilled vine leaves. Pack the rolls tightly into the pan, seam-side-down, in layers. Pour the beef broth over the rolls until they are just covered with liquid; weight with a heavy plate to keep the rolls from opening. Cover and bring to a boil. Reduce the heat to simmer and cook for 30 minutes.

Pour off 1 cup of broth and use to make Egg and Lemon Sauce (see Index).

Serve warm with the sauce poured over. Makes 6 servings.

meat pies
kreatopittes

dough

2 cups flour
2½ teaspoons baking powder
1 teaspoon salt
⅓ cup shortening
¾ cup milk

filling

½ cup chopped onion
¼ cup chopped green pepper
2 tablespoons butter

1½ cups finely chopped
    leftover cooked beef or
    lamb
2 hard-cooked eggs, peeled
    and chopped
1 medium tomato, peeled,
    seeded, and chopped
2 tablespoons chopped parsley
½ teaspoon salt
¼ teaspoon pepper
1 egg beaten with 2
    tablespoons of milk

In a mixing bowl combine the flour, baking powder, and salt. Cut in the shortening until the mixture resembles coarse meal. Add the milk and stir with a fork to form a soft dough. Wrap the dough in plastic wrap and refrigerate it while making the filling.

Sauté the onion and green pepper in butter until limp. Add the meat, hard-cooked eggs, tomato, parsley, salt, and pepper and mix well. Remove from the heat.

On a pastry cloth roll out the dough ¼ inch thick and cut it into 3½ × 5-inch pieces. Top with 3 tablespoons of filling and fold like a pocketbook. Seal with the egg mixture and place on an ungreased cookie sheet. Brush the tops with the egg and milk mixture. Bake at 400°F for 15 minutes or until well-browned.

Serve with garlic-flavored yogurt. Makes 12 small pies or 3 to 5 servings.

Note: Frozen puff pastry can be used for this recipe.

stuffed zucchini

yemistes kolkythia

4 medium zucchini squash
 (about 2 pounds total)
1 pound ground beef
¼ cup olive oil
2 cloves garlic, minced
1 medium chopped onion
½ cup chopped green pepper

1 teaspoon crushed dried mint
1 cup fresh bread crumbs
1 tablespoon chopped parsley
1¾ cups tomato sauce
¼ cup grated Kafaloteri
 cheese
Salt and pepper

Slice the zucchini in half lengthwise. Scoop out the pulp and chop.

Sauté the ground beef in the olive oil until it loses its pink color. Add the garlic, onion, and green pepper and cook for 5 more minutes. Remove from the heat. Add the zucchini pulp, mint, bread crumbs, parsley, ¼ cup tomato sauce, cheese, and salt and pepper to taste.

Stuff the squash shells with the mixture. Put the squash in a 13 × 9 × 2-inch baking dish, and pour the remaining 1½ cups of tomato sauce over the squash.

Bake at 350°F for 40 minutes. Makes 4 servings.

stuffed zucchini

macaroni casserole with eggplant

macaroni casserole with eggplant
makaronada me melitzanes

1 eggplant (1 pound)
4 medium tomatoes
5 tablespoons oil
2 cloves garlic, chopped
½ teaspoon salt
¼ teaspoon pepper
1 stick cinnamon
¼ teaspoon allspice
½ cup red wine
3 tablespoons tomato paste

8 ounces whole or elbow
  macaroni
3 quarts boiling, salted water
3 tablespoons olive oil
1 pound meat-loaf mixture
2 medium onions, chopped
¼ cup grated Kafaloteri
  cheese
2 tablespoons butter

Clean the eggplant and dice into 1-inch cubes.

Peel and quarter the tomatoes.

Heat the 5 tablespoons of oil in a large skillet. Sauté the eggplant, tomatoes, and garlic for 5 minutes, stirring occasionally, to prevent sticking. Add the salt, pepper, cinnamon stick, allspice, wine, and tomato paste. Simmer for 15 minutes.

Meanwhile, cook the macaroni in 3 quarts of boiling, salted water until done. Drain and rinse in warm water.

Heat the remaining 3 tablespoons of oil. Brown the meat and onions. Combine with the vegetable mixture. Remove the cinnamon stick.

Grease a 13 × 9 × 2-inch casserole. Place the macaroni in the casserole. Add one half of the cheese, and mix. Top with the vegetable mixture and remaining cheese. Dot with butter.

Bake at 350°F for 30 minutes. Makes 6 servings.

lamb and green beans
arni me fasolakia

2 tablespoons flour
1 teaspoon salt
¼ teaspoon pepper
6 lamb shoulder chops (2 to
  2½ pounds)
2 tablespoons olive oil
1 large onion, sliced
1 clove garlic, crushed
1½ cups chicken broth

1½ pounds green beans, ends
  nipped and cut in 1-inch
  sections
1 pound small new potatoes,
  scrubbed and a 1-inch strip
  removed around the middle
2 eggs
¼ cup lemon juice
Parsley
Lemon wedges

Mix the flour, salt, and pepper. Coat the chops and shake off the excess.

Heat the oil in a Dutch oven and brown the chops evenly on both sides. Remove from the pan.

Sauté the onion and garlic until soft. Stir in the chicken broth and bring to boiling. Arrange the chops, green beans, and potatoes in the pan. Cover and reduce the heat to low. Cook, basting occasionally, for 45 to 50 minutes or until done. Arrange the chops and vegetables in a large bowl or deep platter and keep them warm.

Beat the eggs until foamy. Add the lemon juice while continuing to beat. Gradually beat in the pan juices and return the sauce to the pan. Cook over very low heat, stirring constantly, until thickened.

Pour the sauce over the chops and garnish with parsley and lemon wedges. Makes 6 servings.

variation
Substitute a 2½- to 3-pound cabbage, cut into 6 wedges, for the green beans. Follow the cooking method as given above.

lamb shanks with rice and green grapes
arni me rizi ke stafeli

2 tablespoons olive oil	¼ teaspoon pepper
4 lamb shanks, cracked	1 bay leaf
½ cup chopped onion	3 tablespoons butter
3 cups chicken broth	1 cup raw long-grain rice
½ teaspoon salt	2 cups green seedless grapes

Heat the olive oil in a heavy skillet and brown the lamb shanks. Place them in a 3-quart casserole.

Brown the onion and add to the lamb shanks. Pour the chicken broth into the casserole and add the seasonings. Cover and cook at 375°F for 2 to 2½ hours or until the meat is fork-tender. Pour off the liquid and keep the lamb warm.

Melt 1 tablespoon of butter in a 1½- to 2-quart saucepan and brown the rice lightly. Add 2½ cups of lamb broth. Cover tightly. Reduce the heat to simmer and cook 20 to 25 minutes or until all the liquid is absorbed.

Meanwhile, melt the 2 remaining tablespoons of butter in a heavy skillet. Just before serving, cook the grapes in the butter, over medium-high heat, until bright green.

Arrange the rice in a large dish, top with the lamb shanks, spoon the grapes and butter over the lamb, and serve. Makes 4 servings.

lamb stew with white beans
arni yahni me fasolia

2 tablespoons olive oil	1 bay leaf
1 pound boneless lamb for stew, cut in 1½-inch pieces	½ teaspoon oregano
	½ cup water
1 cup chopped onion	1½ cups canned tomatoes
2 cloves garlic, chopped	2 tablespoons tomato paste
1 small stalk celery, chopped	2 1-pound cans white beans, drained
2 medium carrots, sliced	
1 teaspoon salt	2 tablespoons chopped parsley
¼ teaspoon pepper	

Heat the oil in a Dutch oven. Brown the lamb on all sides. Add the onion and garlic and continue to cook for 5 minutes, until the onion and garlic are limp. Add the celery, carrots, seasonings, water, tomatoes, and tomato paste. Cover and cook over low heat for 1½ hours. Add the beans and cook for 1 hour or until the lamb is tender.

Garnish with chopped parsley and serve with crusty bread. Makes 4 servings.

lamb and cucumber stew
arni me agouria yahni

2 pounds lamb shoulder	2 medium cucumbers
¼ cup olive oil	2 teaspoons vinegar
2 onions, chopped	1 teaspoon sugar
1 cup canned whole tomatoes	1 tablespoon fresh dill, chopped, or ½ teaspoon dried dillweed
2 cups beef broth	
½ teaspoon salt	
¼ teaspoon pepper	

Wipe the meat with a damp cloth. Remove the meat from the bones and cut into 1-inch cubes.

Heat the oil in a Dutch oven. Add the meat and brown it on all sides. Add the onions and cook until glossy. Add the tomatoes and broth. Season with salt and pepper. Cover and cook over low heat for 45 to 50 minutes or until the meat is tender.

Wash and pare the cucumbers. Cut them in half lengthwise. Remove the seeds and cut the cucumbers in cubes. Add to the stew, and cook 5 minutes. Add the vinegar, sugar, and dill.

Stir to combine, and serve. Makes 4 servings.

roast leg of
lamb bandit-style
bouti arnisio sto fourno tihis

1 leg of lamb (4 to 5 pounds),
   boned, rolled, and tied
2 cloves garlic, cut in slivers
Salt and pepper
2 tablespoons butter
1 3-foot section heavy-duty
   aluminum foil

2 pounds pearl onions, peeled
   and parboiled
2 tablespoons chopped parsley
1 teaspoon dried dillweed
½ cup white wine
¼ cup olive oil
Juice of 1 lemon

Cut slits in the fat on the outside of the lamb roast and insert the garlic slivers. Rub with the salt and pepper.

Heat the butter in a deep skillet. Brown the lamb well on all sides. Place the lamb on the aluminum foil.

Add the onions to the skillet and brown them. Add the parsley and dill, then spoon the mixture around the lamb roast. Pour the wine, olive oil, and lemon juice over the lamb. Fold the foil around the lamb and seal tightly. Place the package in a large roasting pan. Bake at 375°F for 3 hours.

Makes 6 to 8 servings.

cabbage rolls
with sauerkraut
sarmades

1 pound ground pork
1 medium onion, chopped
2 tablespoons olive oil
½ cup raw long-grain rice
1 teaspoon crushed dried mint
½ teaspoon salt
¼ teaspoon pepper
1 large head cabbage
1 1-pound can sauerkraut
2 large tomatoes, peeled and
   chopped
2 cups beef broth
Sour cream or yogurt

Brown the pork and onion in the olive oil in a large skillet. Add the rice, mint, salt, and pepper. Set aside.

Core the cabbage head and, under running water, carefully remove 12 to 15 leaves (depending on the size of the leaves). Discard the limp or damaged leaves.

Bring 2 inches of water to a boil in a Dutch oven. Add the cabbage leaves and steam until limp (about 10 minutes). Drain. Place 2 to 3 tablespoons of filling on each cabbage leaf (according to the size of the leaf) and fold the sides to the center and roll. Secure with toothpicks if desired. Shred any remaining cabbage from the cabbage head.

Place the sauerkraut in the bottom of the Dutch oven and add any shredded cabbage, the cabbage rolls, tomatoes, and broth. Place a heavy plate on the cabbage rolls (this weights them down so that they stay under the liquid in the pot as they cook). Cover and cook over low heat for 1 hour.

Serve topped with the cabbage and sauerkraut from the cooking pot and a dollop of sour cream or yogurt. Makes 4 servings.

liver piquant
sikotakia marinata

1 pound calves' liver
¼ cup flour
½ teaspoon salt
¼ teaspoon pepper
2 tablespoons olive oil
2 tablespoons butter
2 cloves garlic, minced

½ teaspoon crumbled
  rosemary
2 tablespoons lemon juice
¼ cup white wine
1 tablespoon chopped fresh
  parsley

Pat the liver dry.

Combine the flour, salt, and pepper and dredge the liver in the mixture, shaking off the excess.

In a heavy skillet heat the oil and butter together over medium heat. Add the garlic and brown lightly. Remove with a slotted spoon and reserve for the sauce.

Fry the liver in the same skillet until brown. Be sure not to overcook it. The liver should be very slightly pink inside. Remove the liver from the pan and keep it warm.

Remove the pan from the heat and add the garlic, rosemary, lemon juice, and wine. Warm the sauce over low heat, scraping any browned bits from the bottom of the pan. Pour the sauce over the liver and sprinkle with chopped parsley.

Let stand a few minutes before serving to combine the flavors. Makes 4 servings.

roast leg of lamb
bouti arnisio sto fourno

1 5-pound whole leg of lamb
  or sirloin half leg of lamb
Olive oil
3 cloves of garlic, peeled

½ teaspoon rosemary
Freshly ground pepper
Salt

Wipe the meat with a damp cloth. Coat the meat completely with olive oil.

Cut the garlic cloves into 4 thin slivers.

Make "X"-shaped cuts approximately ½ inch long and ½ inch deep at intervals in the fat covering the leg of lamb. Place 1 sliver of garlic in each cut. Fill the cuts with the rosemary. Dust the leg of lamb with freshly ground pepper. Roast it in an open pan, fat-side-up, on a rack at 325°F for 3 hours or to an internal temperature of 180°F on a meat thermometer (for well-done). If you like your lamb pink, decrease the time accordingly.

If desired, scrubbed new potatoes can be added to the roasting pan for the last hour of cooking. Allow 1 potato per person. Be sure to peel a thin strip of skin from the middle of the potatoes before placing in the pan. Other vegetables may also be pan-roasted with the meat; for example, whole carrots (peeled), artichokes, onions, or green beans (whole, with the tips removed).

At the end of the roasting time remove the pan from the oven, add salt to the meat, and let it stand before carving. Makes 6 to 8 servings.

skewered lamb

skewered lamb
souvalaki

¼ cup minced onion
1 clove garlic, minced
3 tablespoons olive oil
3 tablespoons lemon juice
1 teaspoon salt
¼ teaspoon pepper
½ teaspoon crumbled dried
    oregano
1½ pounds leg of lamb or
    lamb shoulder meat, cut
    into 2-inch cubes
16 small boiling onions, peeled
16 mushrooms, cleaned and
    stems removed
2 red peppers, cut into chunks

Combine the onion, garlic, olive oil, lemon juice, salt, pepper, and oregano in a glass bowl or casserole. Add the lamb cubes and stir well. Cover and marinate for 3 to 4 hours (or longer in the refrigerator), stirring occasionally.

Parboil the onions in salted water for 10 minutes. Drain and cool.

Drain the lamb, reserving the marinade. Skewer the vegetables and lamb alternately (lamb cube, onion, mushroom, and then a pepper chunk; repeat). Cook over charcoal or in the broiler about 15 minutes, brushing frequently with the marinade.

Serve with rice. Makes 4 servings.

variation
Substitute cherry tomatoes and green peppers for the red peppers. Skewer the onions and meat alternately. Skewer the vegetables separately, and brush them with marinade. Tomatoes can be grilled only a short time or they will fall off the skewer before the meat is done. Start the meat first and add the skewered vegetables 5 minutes before the meat is finished.

27

veal with vegetables
mosxhari tourlou

2 tablespoons flour
3 tablespoons Kafaloteri or
   Parmesan cheese
½ teaspoon salt
¼ teaspoon pepper
¼ teaspoon nutmeg
1 egg, beaten
½ cup milk
1 pound thinly sliced leg of
   veal, cut into serving-size
   pieces

Flour
6 tablespoons butter
1 eggplant, 1½ pounds
2 tablespoons olive oil
4 tomatoes, peeled and
   quartered
Salt and pepper
½ teaspoon rosemary
Juice of 1 lemon
2 tablespoons chopped parsley

Combine the flour, cheese, salt, pepper, and nutmeg. Add the egg and milk and beat until well-blended.

Wipe the veal with a damp cloth and dredge in flour.

Melt 3 tablespoons of the butter in a skillet until it sizzles. Dip the veal in the flour and egg batter. Fry in the butter until golden. Turn and fry the other side. Remove to a platter and keep it warm.

Trim the stem and cap from the eggplant. Leaving the skin on the eggplant, slice it ¼ inch thick. Pour boiling water over the eggplant and let stand a few minutes. Drain.

Heat the oil in a medium-size skillet. Add the eggplant and tomatoes, salt and pepper to taste, and the rosemary. Steam 10 minutes or until the eggplant is tender. Stir several times.

Arrange the vegetables in a serving dish. Arrange the veal on top of the vegetables.

Melt the remaining butter in the pan in which the veal was cooked until it foams. Add the lemon juice and parsley. Pour over the veal.

Serve with Rice Pilaf (see Index). Makes 4 servings.

pork with celery
hirino me selino

1¼ pounds lean boneless
   pork, cut in 1½-inch cubes
3 tablespoons butter
1 medium onion, chopped
1½ cups water
1 tablespoon fresh dill,
   chopped, or ¾ teaspoon
   dried dillweed

½ teaspoon salt
¼ teaspoon pepper
1 bunch celery
2 eggs
1 tablespoon flour
Juice of 1 lemon

Brown the pork on all sides in the butter in a large saucepan or Dutch oven. Add the onion and sauté for a few minutes. Add the water and seasonings.

Scrub the celery and remove large strings from the outer stalks. Reserve the celery hearts for another use. Cut in 2- to 3-inch pieces and add to the meat. Bring the mixture to a boil. Cover and simmer 1½ to 2 hours. Remove from the heat.

Drain off 1 cup of broth and skim any fat floating on the surface. Allow the meat to cool while making the sauce.

Beat the eggs until light. Add the flour and lemon juice and mix well. Slowly beat in the stock.

Very slowly pour the sauce into the stew, mixing well. Serve immediately. Makes 4 servings.

picture on opposite page:
veal with vegetables

marinated pork roast
hirino marinata

1½ cups red wine
2 tablespoons lemon juice
1 clove garlic, minced
1 medium onion, chopped
½ teaspoon pepper
1 teaspoon crushed coriander

1 4-pound loin pork roast, boned, rolled, and tied
3 tablespoons olive oil
2 tablespoons cornstarch mixed with 2 tablespoons cold water (optional)

Combine the wine, lemon juice, garlic, onion, pepper, and coriander. Pour into a glass or deep ceramic container about the size of the pork roast. Add the pork roast and marinate, covered, for at least 8 hours. Turn frequently. Drain and pat dry.

Heat the oil in a Dutch oven. Add the roast and brown on all sides. Add the marinade. Cover and roast in the oven at 375°F for 2 hours. Uncover and bake for ½ hour more.

Strain the pan juices and thicken, if desired, with 2 tablespoons cornstarch mixed with 2 tablespoons cold water. Slice the roast and serve with fried potato slices. Makes 8 servings.

rabbit with sour cherry sauce
lagous me vissino

2½ pounds frozen white meat of rabbit (or 1 whole rabbit, 2½ to 3 pounds, disjointed)

marinade

½ cup water
1 cup red wine
¼ cup chopped onion

5 peppercorns
1 bay leaf
3 cloves

gravy

4 tablespoons flour
6 tablespoons oil
½ cup chopped onion
2 cloves garlic, minced
¾ cup sliced celery
1 medium carrot, chopped
¾ teaspoon salt
¼ teaspoon pepper

¼ teaspoon crumbled rosemary
1 cup hot stock (or beef broth)
½ cup reserved marinade
⅓ cup coarsely chopped walnuts
½ cup sour cherries, canned
3 tablespoons cherry juice

Skin the rabbit and cut into small, serving-size pieces.

Combine the marinade ingredients in a glass or ceramic container. Add the rabbit and marinate for 24 hours. Drain the rabbit, pat dry, and reserve the marinade. Dip the pieces in flour.

Heat the oil in a large skillet. Brown the rabbit on all sides. Add the onion, garlic, celery, and carrot; cook for 3 minutes. Season with salt, pepper, and rosemary. Add the broth and ½ cup reserved marinade. Cover and simmer 1 hour.

Remove the meat and puree the gravy in a blender, or strain it. Combine the meat, nuts, cherries, and juice, and add to the gravy and reheat.

Taste and season with additional salt and pepper if desired. Makes 4 to 5 servings.

poultry

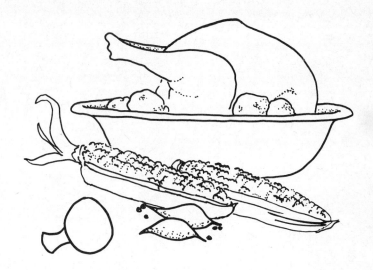

chicken with artichokes
kottopoula me anginares

2 tablespoons butter
2 whole chicken breasts (about 1½ pounds), split
1 clove garlic, minced
½ teaspoon salt
¼ teaspoon white pepper
½ cup chicken broth
¼ cup white wine

1 10-ounce package frozen artichoke hearts, thawed
1 tablespoon cornstarch mixed with 1 tablespoon cold water
3 eggs
2 tablespoons lemon juice
2 tablespoons chopped parsley

Melt the butter in a heavy skillet. Brown the chicken breasts. Add the garlic and sauté for 3 minutes more. Add the salt, pepper, chicken broth, and wine. Cover and simmer for 30 minutes. Add the artichoke hearts and continue to cook for 10 minutes.

Drain off the broth and keep the chicken warm. Measure the broth. One cup is needed for the sauce. Add canned chicken broth if necessary. Heat the broth in a small saucepan and thicken with the cornstarch mixed with cold water.

Beat the eggs well. Slowly add the lemon juice while continuing to beat the mixture. Slowly beat in the hot broth and then return the mixture to the saucepan. Cook over very low heat, stirring constantly, until thickened.

Arrange the chicken and artichokes on a platter. Pour the sauce over the chicken and garnish with parsley. Makes 4 servings.

stuffed chicken–breast athenian

4 split chicken breasts,
  skinned and boned
2 tablespoons crumbled feta
  cheese
1 tablespoon chopped walnuts
1 tablespoon chopped parsley
¾ cup flour
½ teaspoon salt
¼ teaspoon pepper
1 egg
2 tablespoons milk
2 tablespoons olive oil
2 tablespoons butter

Cut a small pocket in each chicken cutlet by making a slit in each piece that does not go all the way through the cutlet.

Mix the feta cheese, walnuts, and parsley. Put 1 tablespoon of stuffing in each cutlet and seal the edges by pressing together.

Mix the flour, salt, and pepper. Dredge the cutlets in the flour mixture.

Mix the egg and milk. Dip cutlets in the egg mixture and then again in the flour mixture. Refrigerate until ready to cook.

Heat the olive oil and butter in a large, heavy skillet, over medium heat, until the foam subsides. Cook the cutlets over medium-high heat until brown. Turn the cutlets over and reduce the heat. Cook until brown and cooked through. Do not cover, as the chicken will lose its crispness and the cheese will begin to ooze out of the cutlet.

Serve the chicken with Rice Pilaf (see Index) and topped with Kima Sauce. Makes 4 servings.

kima sauce

3 tablespoons olive oil
¼ cup chopped onion
¼ cup chopped carrots
¼ cup chopped celery
1 clove garlic, chopped
1 8-ounce can tomatoes,
  drained and chopped
2 tablespoons chopped parsley
¼ cup white wine
¼ teaspoon sugar
¼ teaspoon oregano

Heat the olive oil in a small, heavy skillet. Cook the onion, carrots, celery, and garlic until limp. Add the drained tomatoes, parsley, wine, sugar, and oregano; simmer for 20 minutes or until thick.

broiled chicken with cucumber sauce
kottopoula me saltsa agouria

This makes a great hot-weather meal, since it is light and refreshing and easy on the cook.

¼ cup olive oil
¼ cup lemon juice
1 cup dry white wine
1 teaspoon crumbled dried
  oregano
1 broiler-fryer (approximately
  2½ pounds), split and
  quartered

Combine the oil, lemon juice, wine, and oregano and pour over the chicken in a baking dish. Marinate at room temperature for 3 hours.

Broil in the oven 4 inches from the heat source, turning once, and basting with the marinade, until done (may also be broiled over charcoal).

Serve with Cucumber Sauce. Makes 4 servings.

cucumber sauce

1 cup plain yogurt
⅓ cup olive oil
1 garlic clove, peeled and
  crushed
1 teaspoon salt
1 cucumber, peeled, seeded,
  and finely chopped

Combine the yogurt, olive oil, garlic, salt, and cucumber and serve over the chicken.

chicken kampama
kottopoula kampama

3 pounds chicken parts
2 tablespoons butter
2 tablespoons olive oil
2 medium onions, chopped
2 cloves garlic, minced
1 cup canned tomatoes
½ of a 6-ounce can tomato
 paste
2 sticks cinnamon
¼ teaspoon ground allspice
½ teaspoon sugar
¼ cup red wine

In a large skillet brown the chicken on all sides in the butter and olive oil.
Remove from the pan.

Brown the onions and garlic. Add the tomatoes, tomato paste,
seasonings, and wine. Bring to a boil. Add the chicken. Reduce the heat
to simmer and cook for 1 to 1½ hours or until tender.

Serve with Macaroni Athenian-Style (see Index). Makes 4 to 5 servings.

jimmy's greek chicken

1 5-pound roasting chicken
3 teaspoons dried oregano
1½ teaspoons garlic powder
¾ teaspoon salt
½ teaspoon pepper
1 30-inch piece heavy-duty
 aluminum foil

Wash and dry the chicken. With a sharp knife slash the chicken at 1-inch
intervals on all skin surfaces, down to the bone if possible. This ensures
penetration of the herbs into the meat.

Combine the oregano, garlic powder, salt, and pepper. Rub the chicken
cavity and skin with the herb mixture, using all of it.

Place the chicken in the center of the aluminum foil. Bring the 2 ends of
the foil together over the chicken and fold together several times to seal.
Seal the ends of the foil. Do not fold the foil tightly around the chicken,
as juice will accumulate in the package. Place the package in a roasting
pan. Roast at 400°F for 1½ hours.

Remove the chicken from the oven and carefully open a corner of the
foil. Pour the juices into a measuring cup or gravy boat. Undo the foil
and slice the chicken.

Serve the juices and Rice Pilaf (see Index) with the chicken. Makes
6 servings.

chicken with yogurt
kottopoula me yiaourti

3 pounds fryer-chicken parts
Juice of 1 lemon
Salt and pepper
6 tablespoons butter
2 cloves garlic, minced
2 medium onions, sliced
½ cup white wine
1 cup chicken broth
1 teaspoon crumbled
 rosemary
1 cup plain yogurt
2 tablespoons flour

Rub the chicken with the lemon juice, salt, and pepper.

Melt the butter in a large, heavy skillet. Brown the chicken on all sides.
Add the garlic and onions and brown them lightly. Add the wine, chicken
broth, and rosemary. Reduce the heat to low, cover, and cook for 30
minutes or until the chicken is tender.

Combine the yogurt and flour and mix well.

Remove the skillet from the heat and allow to cool for 10 to 15 minutes.
Add the yogurt and flour slowly, mixing well. Cook, stirring constantly,
over very low heat until slightly thickened.

Pour the sauce over the chicken and serve. Makes 4 servings.

chicken livers and eggplant
sikotakia me melitzanes

1 eggplant (1 pound) peeled and sliced ½ inch thick
¾ cup flour
1 teaspoon salt
½ teaspoon pepper
2 eggs, well-beaten
¼ cup olive oil
2 tablespoons butter
1 medium onion, sliced

1½ pounds chicken livers, washed, drained, and cut in half
2 tablespoons flour
1 cup chicken broth
2 tablespoons white wine
¾ cup canned tomatoes, drained and chopped
2 tablespoons chopped fresh parsley

Soak the eggplant in salted water for 15 minutes. Drain and pat dry.

Combine the flour, salt, and pepper.

Dip the eggplant in the beaten eggs and then in the seasoned flour, coating well.

Heat the oil in a large skillet. Add the eggplant slices and fry over medium-high heat until crisp and brown. Drain on paper towels and keep them warm.

Melt the butter and fry the onion and chicken livers until well-browned. Add the flour, and mix well. Add the chicken broth, wine, tomatoes, and oregano. Cover and simmer 10 minutes.

Arrange the eggplant to form a border around the edge of a large round plate. Put the chicken livers and sauce in the center and top with the parsley. Serve with Rice Pilaf (see Index). Makes 4 servings.

gala stuffed turkey
galapoulo tou fourno

1 16-pound turkey, thawed if frozen
¼ cup lemon juice
Salt and pepper

stuffing

1 stick butter
1 pound ground beef
Liver from the turkey, chopped
1 clove garlic, minced
1 cup chopped celery

1 cup chopped onion
¼ cup chopped parsley
1 teaspoon salt
½ teaspoon pepper
½ teaspoon ground cinnamon
1 cup long-grain raw rice
2 cups water
1 8-ounce can tomato sauce
½ cup currants
½ cup dry white wine
½ cup chopped walnuts
¼ cup pine nuts
½ cup butter, melted

Wash and dry the turkey. Remove the giblets. Reserve the liver for the stuffing. Sprinkle the turkey inside and out with the lemon juice, salt, and pepper.

Next prepare the stuffing. Melt the butter in a large Dutch oven. Brown the ground beef and turkey liver. Add the vegetables, and cook a few additional minutes. Add the seasonings and rice. Add the water and tomato sauce. Cover and cook 20 to 25 minutes or until the rice is tender.

While the rice cooks, soak the currants in the wine. When the rice is tender, add the currants and nuts and mix well. Cool.

Stuff the turkey with the prepared stuffing, and truss. Brush with the melted butter and roast in an open pan for 5 hours at 325°F, brushing frequently with the butter, or until a meat thermometer inserted in the thigh of the turkey registers 185°F. Let stand 15 minutes.

Remove the stuffing and carve the turkey. Makes 12 to 14 servings.

oregano chicken
kottopoula rigani

3 pounds fryer-chicken parts
1 large freezer bag
½ cup olive oil
¼ cup lemon juice
2 cloves garlic, minced
½ teaspoon salt
1 teaspoon crumbled dried
    oregano
½ teaspoon freshly ground
    pepper
2 tablespoons butter, melted

the day before cooking

Wash the chicken parts and pat dry. Place in the freezer bag.

Combine the oil, lemon juice, garlic, salt, oregano, and pepper and pour over the chicken. Tie the bag shut and turn the bag several times to coat the chicken with the marinade. Refrigerate for 24 hours, turning the bag occasionally.

to cook

Remove the chicken from the bag, reserving the marinade. Grill, 5 inches from white-hot charcoal, for 30 minutes, turning once. Brush frequently with the reserved marinade combined with the melted butter. Makes 4 to 5 servings.

variation

Substitute 1 3-pound roasting chicken for the chicken parts. Marinate in the same manner. Drain the chicken, reserving the marinade. Mount on a rotisserie spit, and cook for 1½ hours on an indoor unit or over charcoal. Baste frequently with the marinade mixed with the melted butter.

oregano chicken

35

picture on next pages: roast chicken

roast chicken
kottopoula sto fourno

2 frying chickens, about 3 pounds each
1 teaspoon salt
1 teaspoon freshly ground pepper
2 cloves garlic, crushed
5 tablespoons melted butter

6 medium potatoes, peeled and cut in lengthwise wedges
2 medium onions, peeled and cut in wedges
⅓ cup lemon juice
½ cup water

Wash the chickens and pat dry. Rub with the salt, pepper, and garlic. Place in a large roasting pan, breast-side-up, and brush on all surfaces with 3 tablespoons of the melted butter.

Roll the potatoes in the remaining 2 tablespoons of melted butter and place in the pan with the chicken, along with the onions. Roast at 425°F for 25 minutes. Reduce the heat to 325°F and continue roasting 45 to 50 minutes longer or until the leg joint moves easily.

Pour the lemon juice over the chicken and remove the chicken, potatoes, and onions to a platter and keep them warm.

Skim the fat from the pan juices. Add the water and bring to a boil. Pour into a gravy boat.

Slice the chicken and serve. Makes 6 servings.

stuffed chicken-breast athenian

fish

fish kabobs
psari souvlakia

¼ cup olive oil
¼ cup dry white wine
¼ cup lemon juice
2 cloves garlic, minced
3 bay leaves
½ teaspoon dried oregano
½ teaspoon salt

¼ teaspoon pepper
1¼ to 1½ pounds swordfish or
   halibut steak
2 red peppers, cut in chunks
2 green peppers, cut in chunks
1 onion, cut in wedges
Paprika

the day before serving
Combine the oil, wine, lemon juice, garlic, bay leaves, oregano, salt, and pepper.

Cut the fish into 1½-inch squares and add to the marinade. Cover and marinate in the refrigerator overnight.

to cook
Alternate the fish, peppers, and onions on thin skewers. Dust with paprika and broil for approximately 10 minutes. (May also be charcoal-grilled.)

cocktail sauce

1 cup tomato catsup
2 tablespoons horseradish
½ teaspoon dry mustard

Combine the catsup, dry mustard, and horseradish. Mix to combine well and let stand a few minutes before serving.

Serve the kabobs on a bed of rice and pass the Cocktail Sauce. Makes 4 servings.

fried salt cod
bakaliaros pastos tiganites

1 pound salt cod
1 cup all-purpose flour
1 teaspoon baking powder
1 egg

¾ cup water
1 tablespoon oil
Oil for frying

Soak the salt cod overnight in water to cover. Change the water at least once. Drain the fish. Remove any loose bones and all skin. Cut into serving-size pieces and dry thoroughly with paper towels.

Combine the flour and baking powder. Add the egg, water, and oil. Beat with a mixer or rotary beater until smooth.

Heat fat or oil in a deep fryer or deep, heavy saucepan, using a frying thermometer, to 375°F.

Dredge the fish in a small amount of additional flour. Dip the fish in the batter and fry a few pieces at a time until golden brown and crisp.

Makes 4 servings.

baked fish
psari plaki

1 pound fish fillets (sole, flounder, or red snapper)
1 tablespoon chopped parsley
1 tablespoon lemon juice
¾ teaspoon seasoned salt
3 tablespoons olive oil

1 medium onion, thinly sliced
1 clove garlic, minced
1 large tomato, thinly sliced
3 slices lemon
2 tablespoons white wine

Arrange the fish in an 8- or 9-inch-square baking dish. Sprinkle with the parsley, lemon juice, and seasoned salt.

Heat the oil in a small skillet and fry the onion and garlic until limp.

Top the fish with the onion mixture, including the oil from the skillet. Arrange the tomatoes on top of the onion mixture, then place the lemon slices between the tomato slices. Pour the wine over all and bake at 350°F for 30 to 35 minutes or until the fish flakes with a fork.

Makes 3 servings.

fish with vegetables and yogurt
psari me yiaourti

1 onion, sliced
1 green pepper, sliced
1 tomato, peeled and chopped
1¼ pounds fish fillets
1 clove garlic, minced
½ teaspoon oregano

½ teaspoon salt
¼ teaspoon pepper
3 tablespoons butter
1 cup plain yogurt or sour cream

Place half of the vegetables on the bottom of a greased baking dish. Top with the fish fillets. Sprinkle with the oregano, salt, and pepper. Top with the remaining vegetables and dot with the butter. Bake at 350°F for 30 minutes.

Top the dish with the yogurt, and cook 10 minutes more. Makes 4 servings.

shrimp with feta cheese
garides me feta

1 tablespoon lemon juice
1¼ pounds medium shrimp, peeled and deveined
2 tablespoons olive oil
¼ cup chopped onion
½ bunch green onions, finely chopped (use only part of the green stems)
1 clove garlic, minced

1 cup tomato puree
¼ cup dry white wine
1 tablespoon butter
1 tablespoon brandy or ouzo
¼ teaspoon oregano
1 tablespoon chopped parsley
¼ pound feta cheese, cut in ½-inch squares

Pour the lemon juice over the shrimp and let stand while making the sauce.

Heat the oil in a heavy skillet. Add the onions (green and white) and the garlic, and sauté until limp. Add the tomato puree and wine and let simmer 15 minutes.

Melt the butter and sauté the shrimp until pink (3 to 4 minutes).

Gently warm the brandy. Ignite and pour it over the shrimp. When the flame extinguishes, add the oregano and parsley.

Transfer the shrimp to a small casserole (1½ quart).

Take the remaining juice from the pan in which the shrimp were cooked and mix with the tomato-puree sauce. Pour this over the shrimp. Top with the feta cheese and press the cheese into the sauce.

Bake at 375°F for 15 minutes or until hot and bubbly. Makes 4 servings.

fish and rice casserole
psari pilafi

¼ cup olive oil
½ cup chopped celery
½ cup chopped onion
¼ cup chopped green pepper
1 cup raw long-grain rice
¼ cup chopped parsley
2 tablespoons chopped pimiento
1 bay leaf

½ pound cooked medium shrimp, peeled and deveined
½ pound fillet of sole, cut in 1-inch chunks
2 cups chicken stock
2 tablespoons white wine
½ teaspoon salt
¼ teaspoon pepper

Heat the olive oil in a skillet and sauté the celery, onion, and green pepper until limp. Remove with a slotted spoon.

Add the rice to the oil left in the pan and sauté the rice over medium heat until lightly colored.

Pour the rice and oil into a 2-quart casserole. Add the sautéed vegetables, parsley, pimiento, bay leaf, shrimp, and sole and mix gently. Add the chicken stock, wine, salt, and pepper. Cover and bake at 375°F for 35 to 45 minutes or until all the liquid is absorbed.

Fluff with a fork and serve. Makes 4 servings.

broiled shrimp
garides tis skaras

½ cup olive oil
½ cup white wine
¼ cup lemon juice
2 tablespoons chopped parsley
½ teaspoon crumbled oregano
Lemon wedges for garnish

1½ pounds extra-large
  shrimp, shelled and
  deveined
1 bunch green onions,
  trimmed and cut in 2-inch
  lengths

Combine the oil, wine, lemon juice, parsley, and oregano.

Skewer the shrimp alternately with the onions and marinate in the oil mixture in a shallow pan, turning frequently, for ½ hour.

Broil the shrimp for 2½ to 3 minutes on each side, basting with marinade.

Garnish with lemon wedges. Makes 4 servings.

marinated fish
psari marinata

1¼ pounds rockfish, red
  snapper, or sole fillets
½ cup all-purpose flour
½ teaspoon salt
¼ teaspoon pepper
4 tablespoons olive oil
2 cloves garlic, finely chopped
4 tablespoons wine vinegar
½ teaspoon rosemary

Thaw the fish, if frozen.

Combine the flour, salt, and pepper and dredge the fish fillets, coating well. Shake off the excess flour.

Heat the oil in a large skillet. Fry the fish fillets, a few at a time, until golden brown. Drain on paper towels and keep them warm.

When all the fish has been cooked, add the garlic, vinegar, and rosemary. Stir, scraping up the browned bits in the pan. Cook for a few minutes and then pour over the fish on a platter.

Serve the fish warm or cold. Makes 4 servings.

fried squid
kalamarakia tiganita

3 pounds frozen squid
2 cups bread crumbs
1 teaspoon salt
½ teaspoon pepper
¾ teaspoon oregano
3 eggs, well-beaten
Oil for frying

Thaw the squid. Remove the arms by cutting them from the head; reserve them. Remove and discard the head, chitinous pen, and viscera. Wash thoroughly and drain. Cut the mantle into rings.

Combine the bread crumbs, salt, pepper, and oregano.

Dip the tentacles and mantle rings in the eggs and then in the bread-crumb mixture, coating well.

Deep-fat fry at 350°F until golden brown. Serve immediately with lemon wedges. Makes 4 or 5 servings.

squid athenian-style

squid athenian-style
kalamarakia athenian

3 pounds frozen squid
1 cup chopped onions
1 clove garlic, chopped
3 tablespoons olive oil
2½ cups canned tomatoes,
  chopped

½ cup chopped fresh parsley
½ teaspoon salt
¼ teaspoon pepper
¾ teaspoon crumbled dried
  oregano
¼ cup white wine

Thaw the squid. Remove the tentacles; chop and reserve. Remove and discard the head, chitinous pen and viscera. Wash the mantle well and cut into pieces.

Sauté the onion and garlic in the olive oil until lightly browned. Add the tomatoes, parsley, salt, pepper, oregano, wine, and squid. Cover and simmer for 1 hour or until the squid is tender.

Serve with rice. Makes 4 or 5 servings.

eggs and cheese

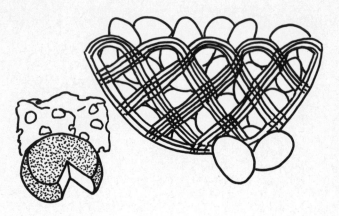

egg pouches
avga me pita

2 tablespoons butter
3 eggs, well-beaten
½ tomato, chopped
2 green onions, chopped

½ cup crumbled feta cheese
½ teaspoon salt
⅛ teaspoon pepper
2 pieces pita bread

Melt the butter in a small, heavy skillet.

Combine the eggs, vegetables, cheese, salt, and pepper. Pour into the skillet and cook over low heat as you would scrambled eggs, until set.

Meanwhile, cut pockets in the bread with a sharp knife. If the bread is large, cut in half and gently separate the inside layers, being careful not to split open the sides. For smaller bread, cut a thin slice from the top edge of the bread and separate the inside layers with a sharp knife.

Fill the bread with the egg mixture and serve with mayonnaise. Makes 2 servings.

artichoke omelet
omeleta anginares

4 tablespoons olive oil
1 clove garlic, minced
2 green onions, chopped
2 teaspoons chopped parsley

1 8½-ounce can artichoke
   hearts, cut in half
4 eggs, well-beaten

Heat the oil in a medium-size skillet or 9-inch omelet pan. Add the garlic and green onions and sauté for 1 minute. Add the parsley and artichoke hearts and sauté for 3 minutes. Add the eggs. Lower the heat and cook until the eggs are set.

Serve with tomato sauce. Makes 2 servings.

egg omelet with green pepper
avga omeleta me piperies

tomato sauce
2 tablespoons olive oil
1 green pepper, cut in slices

1 clove garlic, minced
1 8-ounce can tomato sauce

Make the sauce first. Heat the oil in a small saucepan or skillet. Add the pepper and garlic and sauté for 3 minutes. Add the tomato sauce and lower the heat to simmer. Simmer for 15 minutes.

omelet
4 eggs, well-beaten
1 tablespoon water

Salt and pepper
2 tablespoons butter
½ cup crumbled feta cheese

Beat the eggs with the water; add salt and pepper to taste.

In an 8-inch omelet pan or small skillet heat the butter over medium heat until it sizzles. Add the egg mixture and reduce the heat to low. As the eggs begin to set, carefully lift the edges of the omelet with a spatula and let the uncooked eggs flow to the bottom of the pan. When the omelet is almost done, sprinkle with the feta cheese.

Fold the omelet and serve topped with the Tomato Sauce. Makes 2 servings.

spinach–cheese pie
spanakopitta

1½ pounds fresh spinach
¼ cup olive oil
¾ cup chopped green onions
½ pound crumbled feta cheese
1 cup ricotta or farmer cheese
2 tablespoons grated
   Kafaloteri or Parmesan
   cheese

2 tablespoons chopped parsley
4 eggs, beaten
¼ teaspoon nutmeg
Salt and pepper
1 stick sweet butter, melted
8 ounces phyllo sheets

Wash the spinach well, tear it into bite-size pieces, and discard the stem. Steam the spinach over boiling water for 8 minutes, until it wilts. Drain well and pat dry on paper towels.

Heat the olive oil in a small skillet and cook the green onions for 3 minutes or until limp.

In a large bowl combine the spinach, onions (and the oil from the pan), feta cheese, ricotta, Kafaloteri cheese, parsley, eggs, nutmeg, and salt and pepper to taste. Stir well.

Brush a 13 × 9 × 2-inch baking dish with some of the melted butter.

Brush 4 sheets of phyllo with butter, fold in half, and stack in the pan. Pour in the filling. Stack the remaining phyllo sheets, buttered and folded in half, on top of the filling. Brush the top of the pie with butter.

Preheat the oven to 375°F. Bake 1 hour or until golden brown and puffed.

Cool the pie for 5 minutes and cut into squares. Makes 12 servings.

feta-cheese sandwiches

2 pita-bread rounds
8 ½-inch slices feta cheese
1 cup finely shredded lettuce
½ of a medium tomato, diced
¼ cup diced cucumber

2 tablespoons chopped green
   pepper
2 radishes, thinly sliced
3 tablespoons oil-and-vinegar
   salad dressing

Warm the pita bread. Cut in half and form a pocket in each. Place 2 slices of cheese in each pocket.

In a bowl combine the vegetables and salad dressing.

Stuff each bread pocket with some of the salad mixture, and serve. Makes 2 servings.

rice and pasta

rice with fides
pilafi me fides

1 cup long-grain rice
½ cup crushed fides or vermicelli

3 tablespoons butter or margarine
2 cups chicken broth
1 teaspoon freeze-dried chives

Combine the rice and fides and sauté in the butter or margarine in a 2-quart saucepan until golden brown. Add the chicken broth and chives. Cover tightly and cook 20 to 25 minutes over very low heat, until all the liquid is absorbed.

Fluff with a fork and serve. Makes 4 servings.

rice pilaf with raisins and nuts
pilafi me stafides ke karides

6 tablespoons butter or margarine
1 cup chopped onion
1 clove garlic, minced
1 cup raw long-grain rice
2½ cups chicken broth

2 tablespoons chopped parsley
¼ cup golden raisins
½ teaspoon salt
¼ teaspoon pepper
¼ cup pine nuts

Melt 4 tablespoons of butter in a small skillet. Add the onion and garlic and sauté until golden. Pour into a 2-quart casserole. Add the rice, chicken broth, parsley, raisins, salt, and pepper. Stir well. Cover the casserole and bake at 375°F for 30 minutes or until the liquid is absorbed.

Brown the pine nuts in the remaining 2 tablespoons of butter.

Fluff the rice and stir in the pine nuts before serving. Makes 4 servings.

rice pilaf
pilafia

2 cups chicken broth or 2 cups boiling water + 2 teaspoons
   instant chicken-broth granules
1 cup long-grain raw rice

Heat the chicken broth to boiling and add the rice. Reduce the heat to simmer and cook for 20 minutes or until all the liquid is absorbed.

Fluff with a fork and serve. Makes 4 to 5 servings.

variations

The stock used to make the pilaf should complement the dish with which it is served. For example, if you are serving a dish made with beef, substitute beef broth for the chicken broth in the recipe above. If you are serving the rice with fish, substitute clam juice diluted with water (1 cup clam juice + 1 cup water) for the chicken broth and cook the recipe in the same manner. Garnish with chopped parsley before serving.

rice pilaf with onion
pilafi me kremmithakia

2 tablespoons olive oil
1 cup raw long-grain or
   converted rice
2 cups chicken broth or 2 cups
   hot water and 2 teaspoons
   chicken-broth granules

2 tablespoons green-onion
   tops, thinly sliced
⅛ teaspoon garlic powder

Heat the oil in a medium-size saucepan over medium-low heat. Add the rice and cook until golden in color, stirring occasionally.

Meanwhile, heat the chicken broth to boiling. Add the chicken broth to the rice. Add the green-onion tops and garlic powder. Cover and simmer for 25 minutes or until all the liquid is absorbed.

Fluff the rice with a fork, and serve. Makes 4 to 5 servings.

bulgur-wheat pilaf
pligouri

¼ cup butter or margarine
1 cup bulgur (cracked wheat)
2 cups chicken broth
1 teaspoon salt

¼ teaspoon pepper
Yogurt
Chopped parsley

Melt the butter or margine in a heavy saucepan. Add the bulgur and sauté, stirring constantly, until the butter is lightly browned. Add the broth, salt, and pepper. Cover, and reduce the heat to simmer. Cook for 25 to 30 minutes or until the liquid is absorbed and the wheat is tender. Let stand, covered, for 15 minutes before serving.

Top with yogurt and chopped parsley for garnish when served. Makes 4 servings.

macaroni athenian-style
makaronia athenian

6 ounces macaroni (either
   whole and unbroken or
   elbow macaroni)

¼ cup butter
1 cup grated Kasseri cheese

Cook the macaroni in 3 quarts of boiling salted water, according to the package directions, and drain.

Meanwhile, melt the butter in a small skillet and cook until golden brown.

In a large bowl place a layer of ⅓ of the cheese; add ½ of the macaroni. Top with ⅓ of the cheese, the remaining macaroni, and the rest of the cheese.

Pour the browned butter over all and serve. Makes 4 servings.

vegetables

fried artichokes
anginares tiganites

8 small artichokes
Juice of 1 lemon
4 tablespoons flour
Bowl of cold water
2 eggs
1 tablespoon warm water

¾ cup bread crumbs
2 tablespoons grated
　Kafaloteri or Parmesan
　cheese
Fat for deep-frying

Peel the tough outer leaves from the artichokes. Slice 1 inch off the tips and a small portion of the stem. Cut the artichokes in half lengthwise and remove the purple choke. Scrape the upper portion and stem to remove any dark green.

Add the lemon juice and flour to the bowl of cold water. Drop the artichoke hearts into the bowl as you work. Drain just before cooking.

Parboil the artichoke hearts in boiling salted water 30 to 45 minutes or until tender. Drain well.

Dip the artichoke hearts in the eggs and then in the bread crumbs and then dip them in the eggs and crumbs again. Fry in the hot fat (365°F) until brown.

Drain on paper towels and serve. Makes 4 servings.

variations

Any of the following vegetables can be breaded and fried in the above manner.

Eggplant (1 pound): Cut into slices ½ inch thick. Soak in salted water before breading. Drain, dip in egg and water mixture and then in crumbs. Dip again. Shallow-fry in hot oil until golden.

Squash (1 pound): Cut into slices ½ inch thick. Do not parboil. Bread and deep-fry, using the same method as for the artichoke hearts.

Cauliflower (1 medium head): Clean the cauliflower head, separate into florets, and parboil in salted water until crisp-tender. Drain well. Bread and deep-fry, using the same method as for the artichoke hearts.

baked artichoke hearts
anginares sto fourno

2 8½-ounce cans artichoke
 hearts, drained
4 tablespoons olive oil

¾ cup fresh bread crumbs
Salt and pepper
½ teaspoon paprika

Cut the artichoke hearts in half. Place in a small casserole and sprinkle with 2 tablespoons of the olive oil. Top with the bread crumbs, salt and pepper to taste, and paprika. Sprinkle with the remaining olive oil. Bake at 350°F for 30 minutes.

Serve with Egg and Lemon Sauce. Makes 4 servings.

variation

2 packages (10½ ounces) frozen artichoke hearts (thawed) can be substituted for the canned artichoke hearts.

egg and lemon sauce
avgolemono saltsa

1 cup broth
1 tablespoon cornstarch
1 tablespoon water

3 eggs, separated
¼ cup lemon juice

Use the stock in which the meat, poultry, or vegetables was cooked, or use canned chicken broth. Heat the broth to boiling and thicken with a mixture of the cornstarch and water.

Beat the egg whites until stiff. Add the egg yolks and continue beating. Add the lemon juice slowly while beating. Slowly beat in ½ cup of the chicken broth.

Return the egg mixture to the pot with the rest of the broth, mixing thoroughly. Cook over very low heat until the mixture thickens. Do not boil. Be sure to stir constantly (a wire whisk would be ideal for this purpose) or the mixture will curdle.

Serve with meat, fish, vegetables, or poultry or use to thicken fish or vegetable dishes. Makes 2 cups.

spicy braised potatoes
patates yiahni savori

1 cup finely chopped onion
¼ cup olive oil
4 medium potatoes, peeled
 and sliced

2 tablespoons tomato paste
½ teaspoon salt
¼ teaspoon pepper
Water to cover

In a medium-size skillet sauté the onion in olive oil until browned. Add the potatoes, tomato paste, salt, pepper, and enough water barely to cover the potatoes. Bring to a boil. Reduce the heat to simmer and cook for 30 minutes or until the potatoes are tender. Makes 4 servings.

tomatoes with feta cheese
domates me feta

This recipe makes a delicious first course or an attractive accompaniment for chicken or fish.

4 medium ripe tomatoes
1 cup crumbled feta cheese
1 teaspoon crumbled oregano
Salt and pepper

Slice the tomatoes in half. Use a decorative zigzag pattern if you wish. Sprinkle each tomato half with 2 tablespoons of cheese and some of the oregano, salt, and pepper.

Broil and serve immediately. Makes 4 servings.

braised green beans
fasolakia yiahni

3 tablespoons olive oil
½ cup chopped onion
1 clove garlic, minced
1 pound fresh green beans, washed and the tips removed
1 cup canned tomatoes
1 tablespoon tomato paste
½ teaspoon salt
¼ teaspoon pepper
½ teaspoon oregano
½ cup water (approximately)

Heat the olive oil in a heavy saucepan. Add the onion and garlic and cook until golden. Add the remaining ingredients. The juices should just cover the beans in the pan. If not, add a little more water. Cover and cook over low heat for 45 minutes or until fork-tender.

Serve the beans with the pan juices. Makes 4 servings.

braised green beans and potatoes
fasolakia me patates yiahni

2 tablespoons butter
½ cup chopped onions
1 pound green beans, ends nipped, and cut into 1-inch pieces
4 medium potatoes, pared and cut in ¼-inch slices
1 cup chicken broth
½ teaspoon salt
¼ teaspoon oregano

Melt the butter in a large saucepan and sauté the onions until limp. Add the beans and stir to combine with the onions. Arrange the potatoes on top of the beans. Pour on the chicken broth and sprinkle with salt and oregano. Heat to boiling. Cover and lower the heat to simmer. Cook for 15 minutes or until the vegetables are tender. Makes 4 servings.

green beans plaki
fasoulakia plaki

1½ pounds green beans
¼ cup olive oil
2 medium onions, chopped
Juice of 1 lemon
¾ teaspoon salt
¼ teaspoon pepper
⅓ cup bread crumbs
¾ teaspoon dried savory
1 bunch parsley, chopped
2 cups hot water

Clean the beans, wash, and cut in half.

Heat the oil in a large saucepan. Then layer the beans, onions, lemon juice, salt, pepper, bread crumbs, and herbs, reserving ½ cup parsley for garnish. The last layer should be beans. Add the water. Cook over low heat for 30 to 35 minutes or until the beans are tender. Garnish with parsley and cool.

Serve cold as an accompaniment to a main dish. Makes 6 servings.

spinach and rice
spanakorizo

1 pound fresh spinach
½ cup chopped green onions
¼ cup olive oil
1 cup long-grain raw rice
¼ cup tomato sauce
2 cups water
2 teaspoons instant beef-broth granules (or 2 bouillon cubes)
½ teaspoon salt
¼ teaspoon pepper

Rinse the spinach well. Discard the stems and yellow or damaged leaves. Tear the spinach into bite-size pieces.

Sauté the onions in the olive oil in a large saucepan for 2 minutes. Add the rice and sauté until golden. Add the spinach, tomato sauce, water, beef-broth granules, salt, and pepper. Bring the mixture to a boil. Cover, reduce the heat to simmer, and cook for 20 minutes or until the rice is tender.

Serve as a side dish with meat or fowl. Makes 4 servings.

Picture on opposite page: green beans plaki

stuffed eggplant
melitzanes yemistes

2 small eggplants (about ¾ pound each)
3 tablespoons olive oil
2 tablespoons butter
2 medium onions, thinly sliced
1 pound tomatoes, peeled, seeded, and chopped
2 cloves garlic
½ teaspoon salt
1 bay leaf
1 2-inch stick of cinnamon
¼ teaspoon pepper
½ cup finely chopped parsley
8 black olives
8 anchovy fillets

Remove stems and caps from the eggplants.

Heat the olive oil in a large skillet, add the eggplants, and cook over medium-high heat for 5 minutes. Remove from the pan. Cut in half lengthwise and carefully scoop out the pulp, leaving a thin shell. Chop the eggplant pulp coarsely.

Heat the butter in the same skillet. Add the onions and cook until golden. Add the tomatoes and eggplant pulp and cook for 10 minutes.

Crush the garlic cloves with the salt. Add to the tomato mixture. Add the bay leaf, cinnamon stick, pepper, and parsley and cook for 10 more minutes.

Fill the eggplant shells with this mixture. Garnish each shell with 2 olives and 2 anchovy fillets.

Bake at 375°F for 10 minutes and serve. Makes 4 servings.

stuffed eggplant

tomatoes plaki
domates plaki

1½ pounds tomatoes
4 medium onions
2 bunches parsley
1 bunch fresh dill or 1
  tablespoon dried dillweed
½ cup olive oil

¾ teaspoon dried thyme
¾ teaspoon salt
¼ teaspoon pepper
¾ teaspoon sugar
Juice of ½ lemon

Scald, peel, and slice the tomatoes.

Peel the onions; slice very thin.

Wash and dry the parsley and dill; chop fine. Reserve ⅓ of the parsley and dill for garnish.

Place 1 tablespoon of oil in the bottom of a 2-quart casserole. Layer ¼ of the tomatoes in the casserole. Top with ⅓ of the onions and ⅓ of the parsley and dill. Sprinkle with some of the thyme, salt, pepper, sugar, and 1 tablespoon of oil. Continue layering, ending with tomatoes. Pour on the lemon juice and remaining oil. Cover and bake for 25 minutes at 400°F.

Cool and garnish with the remaining parsley and dill. Serve cold. Makes 6 servings.

eggplants stuffed with rice and meat
melitzanes yemistes me rizo ke kreas

2 eggplants (1 pound each)
Salt
3 tablespoons olive oil
1 onion, chopped
1 clove garlic, minced
½ cup long-grain raw rice
1 cup chicken broth

1 tablespoon chopped parsley
½ cup finely chopped cooked
  beef, ham, or pork
2 medium tomatoes, peeled
  and quartered
4 slices processed cheese

Wash the eggplants and cut in half lengthwise. Cut several deep slits in the flesh. Sprinkle with salt and let stand 15 minutes. Scoop the pulp from the eggplants, leaving a ¾-inch-thick shell. Chop the pulp.

Heat the oil in a medium skillet. Fry the onion and garlic for 3 minutes. Add the rice and sauté for several minutes. Add the chicken broth. Cover, and reduce the heat to simmer. Cook for 20 minutes or until the rice is tender. Remove from the heat. Add the eggplant pulp, parsley, meat, and tomatoes. Mix well and stuff the eggplant shells with the mixture.

Place the shells in an open baking dish. Bake at 375°F for 20 minutes. Top with the cheese slices and bake 10 minutes more.

Serve with a crisp green salad. Makes 4 servings.

zucchini fritters
kololythia krokettes

2 medium zucchini, grated
  (2 cups)
½ teaspoon salt
2 eggs
¼ cup grated Kasseri cheese
½ teaspoon oregano

2 tablespoons all-purpose
  flour
¼ teaspoon pepper
2 tablespoons olive oil
2 tablespoons butter

Mix the zucchini and salt and let stand for 1 hour. Drain well and pat dry with paper towels.

Beat the eggs. Add the zucchini, cheese, oregano, flour, and pepper, and mix well.

Heat the olive oil and butter over medium heat until the foam subsides. Cook the batter a tablespoon at a time, turning to brown both sides.

Serve with tomato sauce. Makes 4 servings (12 pancakes).

breads

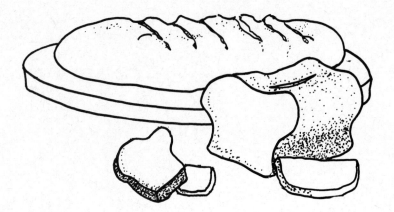

arabic flatbread
pita

This bread, though not truly Greek, makes delicious sandwiches.

1 ¼-ounce package active dry
    yeast
1¼ cups lukewarm (105 to
    115°F) water

3 cups all-purpose flour
1¼ teaspoons salt
2 teaspoons sugar

Dissolve the yeast in the warm water in a medium-size bowl.

Combine the flour, salt, and sugar. Add the flour mixture to the yeast-and-water mixture, stirring to form a sticky dough. Knead well (15 to 20 minutes) on a floured board, adding more flour if necessary to prevent sticking. The dough should be smooth and satiny. Place in a medium-size bowl and cover with plastic wrap and then a towel. Put in a warm place to rise until double in bulk (1 to 1½ hours).

Punch the dough down. Divide the dough into 6 equal pieces, forming each piece into a ball. With a rolling pin, roll each ball into a 5-inch circle on a floured board. Place the circles on lightly oiled pieces of waxed paper. Place on cookie sheets and cover with lightly floured towels. Allow to rise 45 minutes, or until puffed.

Preheat the oven to 450°F. Place the bread on baking sheets or in a preheated cast-iron skillet, by inverting the waxed paper onto the cookie sheet and gently peeling the paper away. Bake for 15 minutes, until browned and puffed. If the rounds are not brown enough after 15 minutes, turn on the broiler unit for 2 minutes to brown. Remove from cookie sheets and wrap in towels to cool. Bread will be hard but will soften as it cools.

Store in a plastic bag. These freeze very well. Makes 6 rounds.

continental bread
psomi

½ cup water
2 tablespoons oil
5 tablespoons milk
1 ¼-ounce package active dry
   yeast
2¼ cups all-purpose flour
½ teaspoon salt
1 egg
2 tablespoons milk
1 tablespoon sesame seeds

Combine the water, oil, and milk in a small saucepan and heat to lukewarm (105 to 115°F). Pour into a small mixing bowl and dissolve the yeast in the liquids.

Combine the flour and salt. Add 1 cup of the flour mixture and beat with an electric mixer for 2 minutes. Add the rest of the flour mixture and stir to form a stiff dough.

Turn out the dough onto a floured board and knead until smooth and elastic.

Lightly grease a mixing bowl with cooking oil and place the dough in it, rotating to oil the entire surface. Cover and remove to a warm place to rise until light and airy (1 to 2 hours).

Punch the dough down. Form it into a round loaf and place on a lightly floured cookie sheet.

Beat the egg with the milk and brush the loaf with this mixture. Sprinkle with sesame seeds. With a very sharp knife cut a cross on the top. Cover and allow to rise until double in bulk and light (1 to 2 hours).

Preheat the oven to 400°F. Put the bread on the middle shelf of the oven and place a small cake pan with 1 inch of hot water in it on the shelf beneath it. Bake for 15 minutes, then reduce the heat to 350°F and bake for an additional 15 minutes.

Remove from the oven and cool on a rack. Makes 1 round loaf.

for rolls

Let the dough rise once. Punch it down. Place on a floured board and divide into 6 equal pieces. Shape and place on a cookie sheet. Brush with egg mixture and sprinkle with seeds. Cover and let rise for 45 minutes or until doubled in bulk and light.

Preheat the oven to 450°F. Place the cookie sheet on the center shelf in the oven and place a cake pan with 1 inch of hot water in it on the shelf just below it. Bake for 10 minutes.

Remove to a rack and cool. Makes 6 rolls.

new year's bread
vasilopita

This cake is traditionally served at midnight on New Year's Eve. The head of the household cuts the cake and the lucky family member getting the coin is said to have good fortune in the coming year.

⅓ cup sugar
4 tablespoons butter
½ teaspoon salt
½ cup milk
1 package active dry yeast
¼ cup warm water (105 to 115°F)
1 teaspoon ground cardamom
2 eggs, beaten
3 to 3¼ cups all-purpose flour
Silver coin wrapped in foil
1 egg, beaten with 1 tablespoon water
Sesame seeds
Blanched almonds

Combine the sugar, butter, salt, and milk in a small saucepan. Heat just until the butter melts. Cool to lukewarm.

In a large mixing bowl dissolve the yeast in the warm water. Add the milk mixture, cardamom, and eggs and beat until combined. Add 1½ cups of the flour and beat for 5 minutes. Stir in enough of the remaining flour to form a soft dough.

Knead on a floured surface for 10 minutes or until smooth and satiny. Form into a ball. Place in an oiled bowl. Rotate the dough to grease the surface. Cover with a towel and let rise in a warm place until double in bulk.

Punch down the dough. Let rise again until almost doubled in bulk.

Punch down the dough again. Form into a 9-inch-round cake, placing the foil-wrapped silver coin in the loaf. Place on a greased cookie sheet. Cover and let rise until double in bulk.

Brush with the egg and water mixture, sprinkle with sesame seeds, and decorate with blanched almonds. Bake at 375°F for 25 minutes or until golden brown. Makes 1 9-inch-round loaf.

desserts

ouzo cake
ouzo keik

1 cup chopped walnuts	4 eggs
1 18½-ounce lemon cake mix	¾ cup water
1 3¾-ounce instant lemon	½ cup cooking oil
pudding mix	¼ cup ouzo

Preheat the oven to 325°F.

Grease and flour a 10-inch tube pan. Sprinkle the walnuts evenly over the bottom of the pan.

Combine the cake mix, pudding mix, eggs, water, oil, and ouzo. Beat for 3 minutes.

Pour the batter over the nuts in the tube pan. Bake for 1 hour.

Place on a rack to cool for 30 minutes. Invert onto a serving plate. Prick with a skewer or meat fork (carefully!!) and pour on the honey syrup.

Let stand at least ½ hour, and serve. Makes 12 servings.

honey syrup

1 cup sugar	2 whole cloves
1 cup water	1 cup honey
1 2-inch piece cinnamon stick	2 tablespoons ouzo

Combine the sugar, water, cinnamon, and cloves. Bring the mixture to boiling, and reduce the heat. Cook for 25 minutes, without stirring, or until the mixture is syrupy (230°F on a candy thermometer). Stir in the honey and strain. Stir in the ouzo.

shredded pastry with nuts and honey
kadaife

This recipe is great for emergencies! Try this when the phyllo sticks together and won't unroll or is too dry to work with.

honey syrup

2 cups sugar

1½ cups water

2 teaspoons lemon juice

½ cup honey

In a saucepan combine the sugar, water, and lemon juice. Bring the mixture to a boil over low heat. Wash down the sides of the pan with a wet pastry brush and cook for 10 minutes. Remove from the heat, add the honey, and allow to cool.

dough

1 pound rolled phyllo dough

2 sticks sweet butter, melted and cooled slightly

With a sharp knife cut across the rolled phyllo dough, cutting it into thin shreds.

In a bowl toss the pastry shreds with the melted butter. Spread ½ of the shreds in a 13 × 9 × 2-inch baking dish.

filling

1½ cups walnuts, finely chopped

¾ cup blanched almonds, finely chopped

¼ cup sugar

1 teaspoon cinnamon

Combine the filling ingredients and sprinkle evenly over the dough in the pan. Top with the remaining dough and butter mixture. Press lightly. Cover with foil and bake at 350°F for 30 minutes. Uncover and bake 15 minutes more or until golden. Remove from the oven and immediately pour on the syrup. Cover and let cool.

Cut into squares and serve. Makes 16 to 20 servings.

yogurt pie
yiaourtopitta

crust

1¼ cups graham-cracker crumbs

¼ cup sugar

¼ cup softened butter or margarine

1 teaspoon ground cinnamon

filling

12 ounces ricotta or farmer cheese

1½ cups plain yogurt

3 tablespoons honey

1 teaspoon vanilla extract

Combine the graham-cracker crumbs, sugar, butter, and cinnamon and press evenly into a 9-inch pie pan. Bake at 375°F for 5 minutes, then cool.

Beat the ricotta or farmer cheese well, then add the yogurt a little at a time, mixing well. Stir in the honey and vanilla.

Pour into the pie shell and refrigerate for at least 24 hours before serving. Makes 8 servings.

Note: This pie is delicious with fresh fruit (blueberries, strawberries, or bananas with lemon juice) on top.

greek nut pastry

greek nut pastry
baklava

honey syrup

1 small lemon	1 2-inch piece stick cinnamon
1 cup sugar	4 whole cloves
1 cup water	1 cup honey

Remove the zest from the lemon (the thin yellow skin only, not the white pith). Squeeze 1½ teaspoons of lemon juice from the lemon and set aside.

Combine the lemon zest, sugar, water, cinnamon stick, and cloves in a heavy saucepan. Bring to a boil. Lower the heat and continue cooking without stirring for 25 minutes. The mixture should be syrupy (230°F on a candy thermometer). Stir in the honey and pour through a strainer into a pitcher or measuring cup. Add the lemon juice. Stir and allow to cool.

pastry

½ pound sweet butter, melted	1 cup finely chopped almonds
1 pound phyllo sheets	½ cup sugar
1 cup finely chopped pecans	1½ teaspoons ground
1 cup finely chopped walnuts	cinnamon

Brush a 13 × 9 × 2-inch baking dish with some of the melted butter. Fold a phyllo sheet in half and place in the dish. Brush with butter and top with another folded sheet of phyllo and brush with butter.

In a small bowl, combine the pecans, walnuts, almonds, sugar, and cinnamon and mix well. Top phyllo with ½ cup of the nut mixture. Top with 2 more folded sheets of phyllo, brushing each with butter. Top with ½ cup of nuts. Continue layering 2 folded sheets of phyllo (buttering each) and nut mixture until 2 sheets of phyllo remain. Fold, butter, and layer them to form the top crust.

With a razor blade cut through the top layers into 24 small rectangles. Bake at 325°F for 50 minutes. Remove from the oven and with a sharp knife cut through all the layers of pastry, using the top layers as a guide, to form individual rectangles.

Pour the cooled syrup over the pastry and cool. Cover and let stand overnight. Makes 24 pieces of pastry.

walnut torte

yogurt cake
keik me yiaourti

1 18-ounce yellow cake mix
4 eggs
½ cup vegetable oil (not olive)
1 cup plain or lemon-flavored
  yogurt
½ teaspoon lemon extract
1 teaspoon grated lemon peel
1 teaspoon ground cinnamon
1 cup chopped walnuts

Grease and flour a 10-inch tube or fluted pan.

In a large mixing bowl combine the cake mix, eggs, oil, yogurt, lemon flavoring, lemon peel, and cinnamon. Blend until moistened. Beat for 2 minutes.

Add the nuts and mix just until combined. Pour into the prepared pan. Bake at 350°F for 60 minutes or until done. Cool 10 minutes and then turn out on a rack to finish cooling.

Slice and serve. Makes 16 servings.

walnut torte
karithopitta

½ pound shelled walnut meats
9 eggs, separated
1 cup sugar
½ cup zwieback crumbs
1 tablespoon grated orange
   peel
½ teaspoon salt
1 teaspoon ground cinnamon

½ teaspoon ground cloves
2 teaspoons baking powder
¼ cup brandy
3 tablespoons water
1 teaspoon vanilla extract
Whole hazelnuts or almonds,
   or walnut halves, for
   garnish

Grind the walnuts through the medium blade of a food chopper. You should have 3 cups.

Beat the egg yolks and sugar until thick and lemon-colored.

Mix the ground nuts, zwieback crumbs, orange peel, salt, cinnamon, cloves, and baking powder. Stir into the egg-yolk mixture. Add the brandy and water.

Beat the egg whites until stiff but not dry. Fold into the nut mixture.

Pour into a greased 9-inch springform pan (or 2 9-inch layer-cake pans). Bake at 350°F for 30 to 35 minutes or until the cake tests done in the center. (Bake the 9-inch layers 20 to 25 minutes.) Cool in the pan. When cold, remove from the pan.

Garnish with vanilla-flavored whipped cream and whole hazelnuts, almonds, or walnut halves. Makes 12 servings.

greek shortbread cookies
kourambiedes

greek shortbread cookies

These cookies are traditionally served at Christmas. The clove in each cookie symbolizes the spices brought to the Christ Child by the Three Wise Men.

2 sticks (½ pound) sweet
   butter
½ cup sifted confectioners'
   sugar
1 egg yolk
½ teaspoon vanilla extract
1 tablespoon brandy
2½ cups flour, sifted and then
   measured

½ teaspoon baking powder
½ cup walnuts, chopped fine
   (almonds may be
   substituted)
48 cloves
Additional confectioners'
   sugar

Let the butter soften at room temperature, then beat with an electric mixer until very light and fluffy.

Sift the sugar into the butter, and cream them. Add the egg yolk, vanilla, and brandy.

Sift the flour and baking powder together. Add the nuts and then the flour mixture and stir to form a soft dough. Knead lightly and chill for several hours.

Form the dough into balls, using a rounded teaspoon of dough for each cookie, and place on an ungreased cookie sheet 2 inches apart. Place a whole clove in each cookie. Bake at 350°F for 15 to 20 minutes or until light brown.

Roll the cookies in powdered sugar while still hot. Cool and store in an airtight container. Be very careful in handling these cookies, as they are very delicate. Makes 4-dozen cookies.

sesame-seed cookies

sesame-seed cookies
koulourakia me sousame

1 cup sweet butter
1½ cups sugar
1 teaspoon vanilla extract
3 eggs
5 cups self-rising flour
½ teaspoon ground cinnamon
½ cup sesame seeds
1 egg beaten with 2
   tablespoons milk

Cream the butter until light. Add the sugar and vanilla and beat well. Add the eggs one at a time and beat well after each addition.

Sift the flour and add to the creamed mixture to form a soft dough. Chill the dough several hours or overnight.

To form the cookies, take a scant tablespoon of the dough and roll into a 3½-inch-long rope. Pinch the 2 ends together to form a doughnut shape. Dip in the sesame seeds and place several inches apart on a greased baking sheet. Brush with the egg beaten with milk. Bake at 375°F for 15 minutes or until lightly browned.

Cool on a rack and store in an airtight container. Makes 6-dozen cookies.

index